T0293886

TREKKING THE ROBERT LOUIS STEVENSON TRAIL

THE GR70 THROUGH THE CÉVENNES/ MASSIF CENTRAL

About the Authors

Nike and Jacint met many years ago on a long coach journey as they both travelled into the unknown to build a new life in a different country. It wasn't long before they became inseparable. Travelling quickly emerged as their favourite activity: they had their first walking holiday in Madeira in 2008 and now wherever they go they try to find the best trails.

Nike went to journalism school and Jacint is a keen photographer. They really enjoy walking in the mountains and would happily spend every day on the trails.

When they followed Robert Louis Stevenson's footsteps through the Cévennes they were mesmerised by the diverse scenery. With their guidebooks and photos they want share their passion for walking with others.

Other Cicerone guides by the authors
Walking in Cyprus
Walking in the Algarve

TREKKING THE ROBERT LOUIS STEVENSON TRAIL

THE GR70 THROUGH THE CÉVENNES/ MASSIF CENTRAL

by Nike Werstroh and Jacint Mig

JUNIPER HOUSE, MURLEY MOSS,
OXENHOLME ROAD, KENDAL, CUMBRIA LA9 7RL
www.cicerone.co.uk

Printed in Singapore by KHL using responsibly sourced paper.
A catalogue record for this book is available from the British Library.
All photographs are by the authors unless otherwise stated.

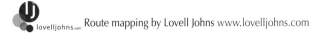

Route mapping by Lovell Johns www.lovelljohns.com

The routes of the GR®, PR® and GRP® paths in this guide have been reproduced with the permission of the Fédération Française de la Randonnée Pédestre holder of the exclusive rights of the routes. The names GR®, PR® and GRP® are registered trademarks. © FFRP 2021 for all GR®, PR® and GRP® paths appearing in this work.

Contains OpenStreetMap.org data © OpenStreetMap contributors, CC-BY-SA. NASA relief data courtesy of ESRI

Acknowledgements

A special thank you to Alison Currier who read some of the stages. A big thank you to Jonathan and Joe Williams for suggesting we explore the GR70 trail.

Front cover: Magnificent views over the Cévennes from the pre-historic burial site (Stage10)

CONTENTS

Note on Mapping

The route maps in this guide are derived from publicly available data, databases and crowd-sourced data. As such they have not been through the detailed checking procedures that would generally be applied to a published map from an official mapping agency, although naturally we have reviewed them closely in the light of local knowledge as part of the preparation of this guide.

Symbols used on route maps

～	route	⌐⌐⌐	track
- - -	alternative route	⌐⌐⌐	vehicle track
Ⓢ	start point	～	tarmac road
Ⓕ	finish point	☕	refreshments
=	bridge	⬆	mid stage accommodation
>	route direction	■	bus stop/bus station
P	parking	*	viewpoint
	woodland	·	other feature
	urban areas		
	regional border		
	international border		
▬■▬	station/railway		
▲	peak		
	tunnel on route		
Ⴑ	campsite		
■	building		
♱ ■ †	church/monastery/cross		
⬚	castle		
⤙	pass		
·	water feature		

Relief
in metres

1600–1800
1400–1600
1200–1400
1000–1200
800–1000
600–800
400–600
200–400
0–200

SCALE: 1:50,000

0 kilometres 0.5   1

0 miles   0.5

Contour lines are drawn at 25m intervals and highlighted at 100m intervals.

GPX files for all routes can be downloaded free at www.cicerone.co.uk/918/GPX.

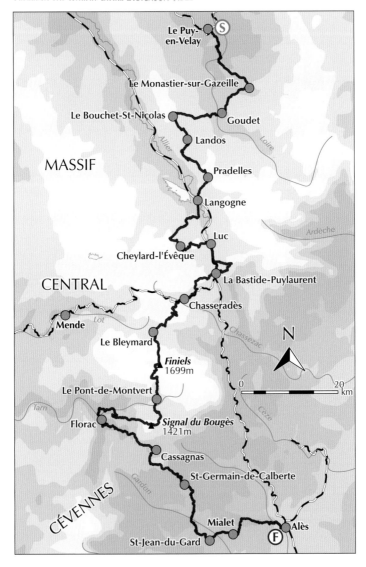

ROUTE SUMMARY TABLE

Stage	Start/Finish	Distance	Ascent	Descent	Time	Page
1	Le Puy-en-Velay to Le Monastier-sur-Gazeille	19km	640m	390m	5hr 30min–6hr	26
2	Le Monastier-sur-Gazeille to Le Bouchet-St-Nicolas	24km	785m	495m	6hr–6hr 30min	35
3	Le Bouchet-St-Nicolas to Langogne	28.5km	395m	690m	7hr 30min	44
4	Langogne to Cheylard-l'Evêque	16.5km	445m	235m	4hr	53
5	Cheylard-l'Evêque to La Bastide-Puylaurent	20km/ 27km	405m/ 675m	500m/ 770m	5hr 30min/7hr– 7hr 30min	60
6	La Bastide-Puylaurent to Le Bleymard	30km	900m	850m	7hr 30min–8hr	68
7	Le Bleymard to Le Pont-de-Montvert	21km	670m	820m	6hr	75
8	Le Pont-de-Montvert to Florac	30km	820m	1180m	7hr 30min–8hr	84
9	Florac to Cassagnas	18.5km	645m	485m	4hr 30min	91
10	Cassagnas to St-Germain-de-Calberte	16km	480m	660m	4hr	96
11	St-Germain-de-Calberte to St-Jean-du-Gard	23km	745m	1055m	6hr	101
12	St-Jean-du-Gard to Alès	25.5km	950m	1010m	7hr 30min–8hr	108
Total		272.5km or 279.5km	7880m or 8150m	8370m or 8640m	12 days	

A faint path leading to a prehistoric burial site (Stage 10)

INTRODUCTION

Magnificent views to Goudet from the Château de Beaufort (Stage 2)

On 22 September 1878, the Scottish writer Robert Louis Stevenson set off from Le Monastier-sur-Gazeille with Modestine the donkey on a 12-day hike through the Cévennes. He kept a journal, and his book *Travels with a Donkey in the Cévennes* – considered a pioneering classic of outdoor literature – was published in 1879. Stevenson would most probably be surprised to see that some 140 years after his journey, many people depart from Le Puy-en-Velay or Le Monastier-sur-Gazeille to walk the GR70 long-distance trail that follows his footsteps as closely as possible.

Stevenson's often-quoted lines beautifully summarise the philosophy of walking that many hikers can identify with:

For my part, I travel not to go anywhere, but to go. I travel for travel's sake. The great affair is to move; to feel the needs and hitches of our life more nearly; to come down off this feather-bed of civilization, and find the globe granite underfoot and strewn with cutting flints. Alas, as we get up in life, and are more preoccupied with our affairs, even a holiday is a thing that must be worked for. To hold a pack upon a pack-saddle against a gale out of the freezing north is no high industry, but it is one that serves to occupy and compose the mind. And when the present is so exacting who can annoy himself about the future?

Back in the 19th century hiking, as such, was unheard of, and Stevenson was often mistaken for a pedlar. Some people even suggested that walking alone might be a dangerous activity – after all, the legend of the Beast of Gévaudan (see Stage 4) still frightened some local people. The writer is believed to have chosen the Cévennes for his walk because he was interested in the area's Protestant history. He recalls some significant events in his book. He also enjoyed talking to local people and he observed their life with interest. And as you walk through the small, peaceful hamlets today, you will see snippets of daily life in rural France. Although it is not clear why Stevenson followed the route described in his book, it is certain that he had to visit settlements in order to get food. This hasn't changed; you will have to stock up in villages, and the stages are planned around available accommodation (see Accommodation).

Robert Louis Stevenson had never hiked before and at the beginning he certainly experienced some difficulties with his four-legged companion.

But he was soon captivated by the amazing scenery.

Some sections of the trail are long and somewhat demanding, so a reasonable level of fitness is required for the trek, which will take you first past tranquil hamlets and endless meadows, and then through mountains and valleys. Extensive views will accompany you along the way. Wildflowers colour the meadows in late May, blackberry bushes dotted with juicy fruit line many paths and tracks in August, and sweet chestnuts are harvested from September to October in the Cévennes. The forest floor is often scattered with wild mushrooms, providing ingredients for tasty local dishes. You can treat your taste buds every day with croissants, coffee, delicious cheese, fresh bread and tasty local wine. For breakfast, your host will probably offer you a selection of home-made jams with fresh bread or toast and coffee, or in many places you can easily get your own fresh breakfast from the local bakery.

Today, locals are used to the number of people with backpacks walking through their villages during

Water troughs are often available for those who travel with a donkey

the summer months, and many places have greatly benefited from the trail; *gîtes* and *auberges* (family-run guest houses) cater for the growing number of walkers.

A whole industry is built around the Stevenson Trail, from companies offering to plan your itinerary, book accommodation and make arrangements for your bags to be transferred, to those offering the option to hire a donkey. You will see both small groups that are part of an organized tour, and solitary hikers staying at campsites and buying food from local grocery shops. However, it is possible and easy to organise and plan everything for your trip by yourself. The GR70 trail is well signposted and it is a great long-distance trail for both first-time and experienced hikers. Every year hundreds of people tackle

the trail in different ways and for different reasons. And as you cross this unforgettable landscape, you will no doubt enjoy some friendly hospitality, sample some local food, talk to fellow hikers, and admire the unique scenery.

ABOUT ROBERT LOUIS STEVENSON

Robert Louis Stevenson was born in Edinburgh on 13 November 1850. The only child of Thomas and Margaret Stevenson, he suffered from ill health throughout his childhood. To ease the symptoms of his illness, he spent time with his mother in the warmer regions of France. Following in the footsteps of his ancestors and his engineer father, Robert Louis Stevenson went to study engineering at the University of

Edinburgh. He showed no interest in the subject but enjoyed travelling with his father to visit lighthouses during the holidays. His appetite for travel might have emerged from these trips and from his childhood years.

In 1871 he admitted to his parents that he had no desire to become an engineer and wanted to dedicate his life to writing. It was agreed that he would study law instead of engineering; he graduated but never practised law. He rebelled against his upbringing in many other ways as well: he kept his hair long, wore bohemian clothes and became an atheist.

In 1873 Stevenson became friends with Slade Professor of Fine Art Sidney Colvin, who was soon to become his literary adviser and who helped get his early works published in magazines. The two remained friends and Stevenson dedicated *Travels with a Donkey* to the professor.

Stevenson travelled to France several times and visited art galleries and theatres in Paris. With his friend Sir Walter Simpson he took a canoeing trip through Belgium and France, and that journey provided the basis for his first travelogue: *An Inland Voyage* (1878).

It was after that trip, in September 1876, that he met Fanny Osbourne in an art colony in Grez. She was 10 years older than Stevenson and, separated from her husband, was living in France with her two children. Stevenson fell in love with her and they spent a lot of time together. In

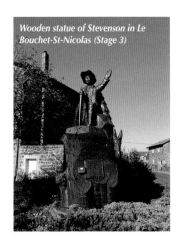

Wooden statue of Stevenson in Le Bouchet-St-Nicolas (Stage 3)

1878, Fanny returned to San Francisco to seek a divorce from her husband, leaving her lover in France.

During this time, maybe to distract himself, and also to collect material for his second book, Stevenson walked with a donkey named Modestine from Le Monastier-sur-Gazeille to St-Jean-du-Gard. The following year (1879) saw the publication of his first successful book, *Travels with a Donkey in the Cévennes*, still in print today. Later that same year he left for California to join Fanny. The story of his journey from Europe to New York appeared in the pages of the *The Amateur Emigrant*.

Fanny and Robert Louis Stevenson were married in May 1880. Between 1880 and 1887, Stevenson experienced problems with his health again, but during that time he also visited Switzerland, southern France and Bournemouth and wrote many of his well-known books, such as the classic *Treasure Island* (1883), *A Child's Garden of Verses* (1885) and *Kidnapped* (1886). In 1888 Stevenson chartered a yacht and, with his mother, Fanny and his stepson, set off to travel the South Pacific. In 1890 he bought an estate on the island of Upolu in Samoa where he died at the age of 44 in 1894. He was buried on Mount Vaea on Upolu.

Read more about Robert Louis Stevenson, his work and legacy at www.robert-louis-stevenson.org.

THE TRAIL

In southern France, the GR70 trail starts from Le Puy-en-Velay running through the Massif Central and finishing at Alès.

The first part of the 272km trail runs through Velay, the landscape dominated by many *puys* (volcanic hills). The trail meanders through fields and past hamlets, gently easing you into the walking. At Langogne, you enter the Lozère area and then the Cévennes, near Le Bleymard.

The second part of the trail traverses the Cévennes – the southeastern part of the Massif Central – and is noticeably hillier than the first part. The Cévennes consist mainly of granite and schist and are characterised by wooded hillsides and some deep gorges carved into limestone by the main rivers. The highest point is the summit of Mont Lozère, Pic de Finiels (1699m), which is encountered about halfway along the trail. Chestnut trees populate the hills near Florac, and sweet chestnuts are harvested every autumn and are used in myriad ways in local products.

Many of the roads have been paved since Robert Louis Stevenson made the journey. Today, the GR70 follows the original route as closely as possible on trails that connect the towns visited by Stevenson. Between Le Pont-de-Montvert and Florac, the GR70 takes you over the mountains and differs significantly from Stevenson's route, which followed the river. It is not known why he chose this route although he did have to visit settlements for food, and he was also interested in the Protestant history of the region (see Stage 7).

PUY LENTILS

The Le Puy-en-Velay area enjoys a warm and dry microclimate and its fertile volcanic soil creates perfect conditions to grow the famous puy lentils, introduced to the area by the Romans some 2000 years ago. Today, the puy lentil has AOP (Appellation d'Origine Protégée) designation, meaning the name can only be used if the lentil is grown in the region. Unlike other types of lentil, the small, dark puy lentil keeps its shape after cooking.

TREKKING WITH A DONKEY

You can hire a donkey to accompany you on the trail but bear in mind that most donkeys can be a lot like Modestine: stubborn and slow. Your four-legged companion might carry your gear but in return you will have to be patient and look after the animal. You can check which accommodation hosts donkeys along the trail in the booklet 'Travels in the Cévennes', which is download-able from www.chemin-stevenson.org.

WHEN TO GO

There are only a few months when walkers can tackle the GR70, as most accommodation is only available from around Easter to October and is closed during the winter months. A good part of the trail runs around and above 1000m, so be prepared to experience variable weather at any time of year. Snow is common during the winter months and May can still be cold; you might experience some very hot days in July and August, while colder and some rainy days are common in September. But the weather can vary from one year to the next.

SUGGESTED ITINERARY

This suggested itinerary, the most popular breakdown of the trail, follows the stages that appear in this book; however, it is possible to plan

Views towards Château de Bouzols on the hill (Stage 1)

your own itinerary differently. There is one long day (Stage 8: Le Pont-de-Montvert to Florac, 30km) that can't be shortened due to the lack of settlements/accommodation along the way, but otherwise you can almost always alter the stages. Your itinerary will depend mainly on the type of accommodation you choose. There are some *gîtes* in between the recommended stages and, if you want to camp, there are campsites along the trail. Some of the stages can be divided into two shorter days.

The recommended 12 stages include the first and last sections from Le Puy-en-Velay to Le Monastier-sur-Gazeille and from St-Jean-du-Gard to Alès. These were not part of the original GR70 trail; however, most people start the trek from Le Puy-en-Velay, and the last section between St-Jean-du-Gard and Alès is now signposted with GR70 signs. But you can make the trek shorter by starting from Le Monastier-sur-Gazeille and finishing at St-Jean-du-Gard (just as Robert Louis Stevenson did).

In some parts of the trail you can join two stages together, but this is not always the case as some stages are already a full day's walk. In the same way, there are stages that can be divided if you want to have some shorter, easier walking days. Each stage finishes in a village where accommodation can be found, although there are some *gîtes* and campsites in other villages and hamlets along the trail. It is always advisable to book accommodation in advance if you are not camping, as the trail is popular throughout the summer.

Suggested itinerary as it appears in this guidebook

- Stage 1: Le Puy-en-Velay to Le Monastier-sur-Gazeille
- Stage 2: Le Monastier-sur-Gazeille to Le Bouchet-St-Nicolas
- Stage 3: Le Bouchet-St-Nicolas to Langogne
- Stage 4: Langogne to Cheylard-l'Évêque
- Stage 5: Cheylard-l'Évêque to La Bastide-Puylaurent
- Stage 6: La Bastide-Puylaurent to Le Bleymard
- Stage 7: Le Bleymard to Le Pont-de-Montvert
- Stage 8: Le Pont-de-Montvert to Florac
- Stage 9: Florac to Cassagnas
- Stage 10: Cassagnas to St Germain-de-Calberte
- Stage 11: St Germain-de-Calberte to St-Jean-du-Gard
- Stage 12: St-Jean-du-Gard to Alès

Stevenson's itinerary in 1878 (based on his journal)

- Day 1 (22 September): Le Monastier-sur-Gazeille to Le Bouchet-St-Nicolas
- Day 2 (23 September): Le Bouchet-St-Nicolas to Langogne
- Day 3 (24 September): Langogne to near Fouzilhic

- Day 4 (25 September): Fouzilhic to Luc
- Day 5 (26 September): Luc to Notre Dame des Neiges (near La Bastide-Puylaurent)
- Day 6 (27 September): Notre Dame des Neiges to Chasseradès
- Day 7 (28 September): Chasseradès to Mont Lozère
- Day 8 (29 September): Mont Lozère to Tarn Valley (beyond Le Pont-de-Montvert)
- Day 9 (30 September): Tarn Valley to Florac
- Day 10 (1 October): Florac to Mimente Valley
- Day 11 (2 October): Mimente Valley to St-Germain-de-Calberte
- Day 12 (3 October): St-Germain-de-Calberte to St-Jean-du-Gard

TRAVELLING TO AND FROM THE TRAIL

There are plenty of flights from the UK and the rest of Europe to Lyon, the closest airport to Le Puy-en-Velay. Easyjet and British Airways offer flights from various UK airports. You can also take the Eurostar to Paris and then continue with the high-speed TGV rail service to Lyon. As always, shop around for the best deals. From Lyon Airport there is a frequent tram service to the city, from where you can take a train to Le Puy-en-Velay (2hr 10min–2hr 30min). There are several trains daily, bookable at www.sncf.com.

Most walkers start the trail from Le Puy-en-Velay; however, if you are short on time or if you prefer, you can skip this first section and start walking from Le Monastier-sur-Gazeille just as Stevenson did. (From Le Puy you can take a bus or taxi to Le Monastier.)

Stevenson took a coach from St-Jean-du-Gard to Alès and, while some walkers do the same, many choose to walk this last – sometimes difficult but very scenic – section. The trail has recently been altered and re-signposted between Mialet and Alès and now it is officially part of the GR70 trail. When you reach Alès, you can take a train (via Nîmes) back to Lyon. Trains run about every 2hr and the journey time is between 2hr and 2hr 30min.

There are also flights to and from Nîmes from some UK and European airports, so you can fly out to Lyon and back from Nîmes, but it is most probably cheaper to book a return flight to Lyon. Alternatively, you can book a return flight to Nîmes, starting your walk with a longer train journey. The journey from Nîmes to Le Puy is about 4hr 30min and you will have to change once or twice.

Another option is to walk only part of the trail, but you will have to arrange transport. It is possible to travel back to Le Puy from Langogne by train. From La Bastide-Puylaurent there are buses to Langogne, Alès and Nîmes, and trains to Nîmes and Alès. From Florac there are buses to Alès. You also have the option of finishing the trek in St-Jean-du-Gard (just as Stevenson did), from where you can take a bus to Alès.

ACCOMMODATION

You are most likely to spend a night in a *gîte d'étape*, an *auberge* (inn/guest house) or a family-run *chambre d'hôtes*. There are some small – often basic – hotels and good campsites along the trail as well. You will have limited choice on some sections where there might only be one or two places to spend the night.

Gîtes provide dormitory-style accommodation; however, some have double rooms as well. Traditionally, they have a kitchen where you can prepare food. If you are planning to stay in a shared room, carry a sleeping bag. Many *gîtes* provide linen, but make sure you have this information when booking. *Chambres d'hôtes* are similar to bed and breakfasts but many offer home-cooked evening meals as well. In reality, places often offer a combination of different types of accommodation.

The Stevenson Trail is becoming more and more popular, so it is highly recommended that you book your preferred accommodation before your trip. It is especially important in the middle section of the trail, where there are few places to stay in the small villages. Most accommodation is available from around Easter to October and is closed over the winter months.

If all accommodation is fully booked in a given village, you may be able to book something nearby, as many of the neighbouring villages cater for walkers as well. You

The trail leads through the pretty village of Chasseradès (Stage 6)

can sometimes alter the stages given in this book to meet your needs. You will see *gîte*, hotel, snack bar and restaurant adverts on trees or lamp-posts along the trail. And for those who plan to camp, there are camp-sites along the trail too. See a list of relevant campsites in Appendix C. While some hikers might choose to camp every night, others will camp some days and spend other nights in *gîtes* or *auberges*. Wild camp-ing is not permitted in the Cévennes National Park.

There is a very handy leaflet, updated annually, with a list of *gîtes* and *chambres d'hôtes* along the trail that you can download from www.chemin-stevenson.org. Most of the *gîtes* and hotels can be booked on www.booking.com or by contact-ing them through their websites. You

can also check www.airbnb.co.uk for alternatives. Details of *gîtes*, *auberges* and *chambres d'hôtes* are given at the end of each stage.

FOOD AND SUPPLIES

There are supermarkets in Le Puy-en-Velay, Le Monastier-sur-Gazeille, Langogne, Le Bleymard, Florac, St-Jean-du-Gard and Alès. These are usually closed on Sundays. You can find bakeries and small village shops where you can buy picnic supplies and some essentials in Le Bouchet-St-Nicolas, Landos, Pradelles, La Bastide-Puylaurent, Le Pont-de-Montvert, St-Germain-de-Calberte and St-Étienne-Vallée-Française. Some village shops close in the mid-dle of the day for lunch and reopen in the afternoon.

There are no shops between Langogne and La Bastide-Puylaurent or between Florac and St Germain-de-Calberte, so you will need to stock up for two days in Langogne and also in Florac.

Most places you stay in can provide breakfast and/or an evening meal. These are often served at a long communal table, giving you the chance to share stories from the trail with fellow walkers. *Tables d'hôtes* offer a set menu for a set price; the time for the meal is often set as well. The booklet 'Travels in the Cévennes' (downloadable from www.chemin-stevenson.org) lists the different services that each place offers.

WHAT TO TAKE

Carry only the essentials and take as little as possible, as on any trek. Take a fleece and waterproof jacket as part of your hiking gear, as the evenings can be cool in the Cévennes, even in summer. Your hiking boots/shoes will be the most important piece of gear, so make sure that they are comfortable and reliable. You might want to take a pair of hiking sandals or flip flops for the evenings to give your feet a break from the boots. You will benefit from taking lightweight hiking clothes that you can rinse in the evenings.

If you are staying in *gîtes*, you should take a sleeping bag; a small travel towel is also advisable as they are not always provided. Sun cream and sun hat are essential, and make sure you carry ample water for the day.

To lighten the weight of the rucksack, many hikers use their phones to take photos, and don't carry a camera. But if you can, take a copy of Robert Louis Stevenson's book: *Travels with a Donkey in the Cévennes*. It is very

Walkers descending from Finiels (Stage 7)

interesting to read the relevant pages each night and see what happened to Stevenson and his donkey Modestine on any given stage.

If camping, you will need standard lightweight camping equipment: tent, sleeping bag, sleeping mat, torch and cooking utensils.

LANGUAGE

If you speak some basic French then you will have no problems on the trail. In rural France most people only speak French and those who have some knowledge of English might prefer to keep it a secret. However, locals welcome hikers and tourists and you can get by with a few French words combined with English and sign language. Appendix D is a glossary of some basic French words that you might find useful.

MAPS AND WAYMARKING

The GR70 long-distance trail is well waymarked with red and white stripes. There are also many different signs, especially at junctions, to help you to follow the route. A red and white cross marks the wrong way at junctions and turn-offs. At junctions, where there are other GR trails crossing the GR70, look out for the GR70 signs. You can also spot some old and some home-made signs. The distances given on some signs might not be accurate. As the trail is well signposted, the maps in this guide should probably

suffice. If you do want a map, take the Stevenson Trail IGN GR70 trail map (1:100,000, 1cm=1km). If you decide to take IGN walking maps (1:25,000) you will need a collection of nine maps to cover the areas. You can download the IGNrando app from www.ignrando.fr.

Google maps or Maps.me applications on your smartphone are also worth considering. Some map apps work offline as well.

GPX tracks

GPX tracks for the routes in this guidebook are available to download free at www.cicerone.co.uk/918/GPX. A GPS device is an excellent aid to navigation, but as the trail is well signposted you most probably won't need one. GPX files are provided in good faith, but neither the author nor the publisher accepts responsibility for their accuracy.

USING THIS GUIDE

From Le Puy-en-Velay to Alès the trail is divided into 12 recommended stages. An information box at the start of each stage provides the following information: start and finish point; distance of the stage; total ascent and descent; the length of time the stage is likely to take; and details about

(Clockwise from top left) direction markers; GR waymarking; right way; Stevenson village sign; turn left, turn right signs; wrong way

A stony path leads downhill to Le Pont-de-Montvert (Stage 7)

refreshments and facilities. Snack bars and shops are mentioned if there are any in a village the trail passes through, but bear in mind that they may be closed and make sure you always carry enough food for the day. Drinking fountains in settlements are mentioned too, but you cannot rely on them, so always carry plenty of water.

The times provided – both for the stages themselves and between intermediary landmarks – are approximate and do not take account of longer breaks for picnics or visiting sights. Once you have started the trek using this guide, you will be able to see how your own pace compares to the times given and you can adjust your planning accordingly.

A couple of accommodation options are mentioned at the end of each stage description, but in many places there are plenty of other

options to choose from and it is highly recommended that you do your own research before booking. The downloadable booklet, 'Travels in the Cévennes' (www.chemin-stevenson. org) lists accommodation available along the trail or you can also look online. Most of the *gîtes*/hotels can be booked on www.booking.com as well. However, there are some small villages where you can only choose from two or three places and to make a reservation you might have to contact them by email.

At the end of each stage there is a short summary of Robert Louis Stevenson's journey on the given section but the best way to immerse yourself in his journey is to read his travelogue: *Travels with a Donkey in the Cévennes*.

THE GR70

Some sections on the trail can be very narrow (Stage 12)

STAGE 1
Le Puy-en-Velay to Le Monastier-sur-Gazeille

Start	Cathedral, Le Puy-en-Velay
Finish	Le Monastier-sur-Gazeille
Distance	19km
Total ascent	640m
Total descent	390m
Time	5hr 30min–6hr
Refreshments	Plenty of cafés, restaurants and supermarkets in Le Puy; bar/restaurant and small shop near the bridge in Coubon; taps with drinking water on either side of the bridge over the Loire in Coubon; supermarket, bakery and small restaurants in Le Monastier-sur-Gazeille

Robert Louis Stevenson didn't start his walk in Le Puy-en-Velay, although he did visit the town before his journey. Today, it is the starting point for many walkers. You might want to spend some time wandering through the cobbled streets and visiting some of the sights before you set off. This first section of the trail eases you gently into the walking and, despite not being officially part of the trail, it is well signposted, and you will see Chemin Stevenson GR70 signs.

LE PUY-EN-VELAY

It is worth spending at least an afternoon in Le Puy-en-Velay. Towering over the town on a hill, the Roman Catholic Cathédrale Notre-Dame du Puy dominates the centre. Its distinctive striped façade is made of white sandstone and black volcanic breccia. Built in the 12th century, the cathedral is a UNESCO World Heritage Site and one of the starting points for the Camino de Santiago pilgrimage. Some mornings you might see pilgrims gathering to be blessed.

Perched on the hill, the iron statue of the Virgin Mary (Notre-Dame de France) was made from 218 Russian cannons taken during the Siege of Sevastopol (1854–55). You can climb the steps inside the statue to enjoy great views of the town.

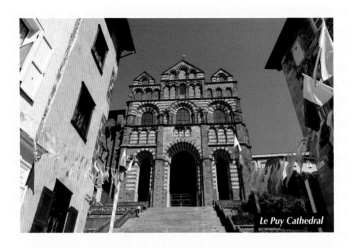

Le Puy Cathedral

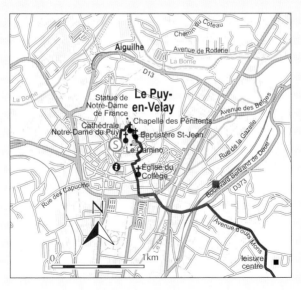

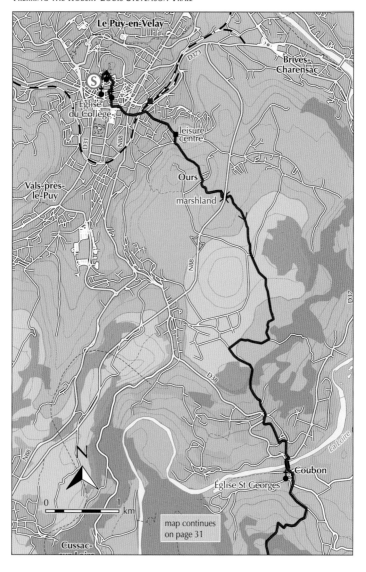

map continues
on page 31

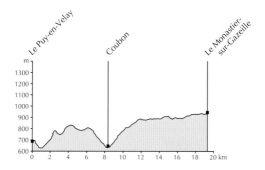

Facing the **cathedral** at the end of the rue des Tables, go left and follow the red and white signs along a cobbled road that skirts behind the cathedral. Go down some steps near the **Le Camino** museum (www.lecamino.org). There are signs indicating the way. Pass the church of St Jean François Regis and, at the next junction, continue straight on downhill.

Reaching boulevard Maréchal Fayolle, go left and, at the junction, turn right onto avenue Georges Clemenceau, passing a World War 1 memorial. Cross the bridge over **Le Dolaizon** and continue uphill by a supermarket on rue Pierre Farigoule. There are views towards Le Puy Cathedral and the Notre-Dame de France statue perched on some rocks on the left. Follow the road over the railway and then continue straight on. Keep right on avenue d'Ours Mons uphill. Turn right just before reaching the **leisure centre** and then immediately left uphill on rue Edouard Estaunié.

Go up the hill with the leisure centre on your left. The tarmac road eventually becomes a path – red and white stripes mark the way – and views open up towards Le Puy-en-Velay with the hills in the background. Walk alongside a stone wall, past a stone cross until you reach a small junction at a hamlet. Carry straight on, go over the road by the cross and then continue downhill on the Chemin du Vallon.

Near the hamlet of Ours, the views are dominated by meadows, fields and hills

Leaving the houses of **Ours** behind, pass a trough and follow the tarmac road. You'll see a small area of **marshland** with a sign on the right. Continue along the surfaced road and, when it splits, keep right and go under the main road (**N88**). After the **tunnel**, cross a surfaced road and follow the sign right on a narrow path lined with blackberry bushes. There is a drystone wall alongside the path as you continue uphill and soon views of fields open up on the right. Joining a tarmac road, turn left and, a few metres later, leave it to the right. Walk first between several fields, ignoring a path on the left, then, shortly after, pass a dirt track on the left and follow the sign straight on. The dirt track becomes a surfaced road. Turn right onto a dirt track and head towards some buildings on the hillside. At the junction, turn right, head towards the buildings and go left by the warehouse. Continue along the red and white-marked stony track. Pass a building with a vegetable garden on the right. The views are dominated by meadows and hills. Notice a cross and bench near the path and, ignoring a path opposite the cross, descend through forest. Also ignore a narrow path on the right as you walk towards a hamlet.

When you reach a paved road by the first house, descend between some houses and, at the road junction with trail signs and a map, facing the map board, keep left. You will reach a main road (**D38**) where you go left on a smaller tarmac road, Route de la Chabanne. Shortly after you will see a red and white sign. Follow the tarmac road steeply downhill and at the junction (Lot Les Mourges) go right as the Coubon sign indicates. **Coubon** is built on the banks of the Loire. At the junction with a bridge, about 2hr after setting out from Le Puy, keep right and then cross the bridge over the **Loire**. ▶

This is a picturesque crossing with views towards the Château de Bouzols on the hill. Église St Georges is on the right just after the bridge.

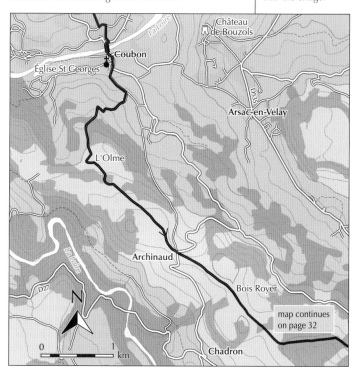

map continues on page 32

31

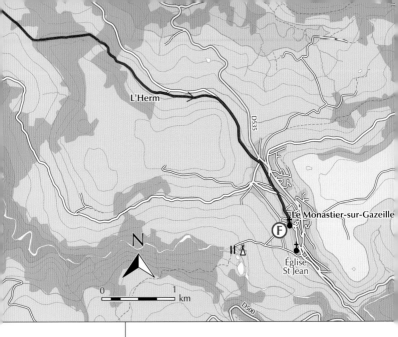

After the bridge, follow the road straight on. Carry straight on on a tarmac road alongside a stone wall at a bend in the road. Ignore a road on the right, pass some more houses and continue uphill on the tarmac road, as the signs indicate. At the road junction, keep right uphill. Pass a cemetery enclosed by hedges. Follow the tarmac road and soon you will pass a small cross on the left.

On reaching the hamlet of **L'Olme** (about 45min after crossing the bridge) follow the tarmac road. Keep left on a gravel road indicated by a Chemin de Stevenson trail sign and walk alongside some fields. There are views to the hills with a small group of houses at the foot of the hill. The track becomes a surfaced road and you continue straight on, as the red and white sign indicates.

At the **Archinaud** road junction continue straight on towards **Bois Royer**, also indicated on red and white signs. Pass some houses (on a surfaced road) with views towards other houses scattered over the slope. After a lone building, turn right on the dirt track. Ignore a path on the right and, when the dirt track splits, carry straight on (as the red and white sign indicates) ignoring two further tracks on the right. Walk through a wooded area, ignoring any sidetracks. When you reach a road with a gate on the right, cross over and carry straight on along a stony path. ▶ Follow the forest track and shortly you will reach some houses and notice a wooden Stevenson sign.

At a minor junction in the hamlet of **L'Herm**, go right as the red and white 'Monastier 3.4 km' sign indicates. Pass some houses then walk uphill among moss-covered rocks. Follow the stony path alongside a drystone wall and shortly you will arrive at a gravel road where you turn left, heading towards the hamlet. When you arrive at a road, turn left again and, a few metres later, follow the sign to the right. Walk between some houses and past an old cross. Pass a *gîte* (Mountcalm) and then carry straight on. At the junction with a playground, continue straight on as the Monastier sign indicates. Soon you'll hear the sounds of the village below you as you descend on the narrow path with views towards **Le Monstier-sur-Gazeille**. When you reach the asphalt road, there is a supermarket on the left where you can stock up with supplies for the following day. Follow the signs to the village centre.

There is an information board about basalt rock, which is prevalent in this area.

Walkers starting their descent to Le Monastier-sur-Gazeille

File dans ta chambre (*gîte d'étape*), 25 rue St-Pierre, **https://filedanstachambre.monsite-orange.fr**, filedanschambre@outlook.fr, tel +33 (0)6 74 59 22 72

Auberge les Acacias, 1 rond-point des Acacias, **www.aubergelesacacias.fr**, aubergelesacacias@orange.fr, tel +33 (0)4 71 08 38 11

STEVENSON'S PREPARATION

Stevenson spent about a month in Le Monastier-sur-Gazeille before setting off on his journey. During that time, he made several trips to Le Puy, where he bought some equipment for his journey. He decided to take a sleeping bag that he would use as a storage bag during the day. It was bulky and heavy, a far cry from the sleeping bags we use today. So Stevenson decided to get a donkey to help carry his heavy bag. He named the donkey Modestine. He packed some warm clothes, books and some food, an empty bottle for milk and, for some unexplained reason, an egg whisk. The residents of Le Monastier thought that Stevenson's plan to walk through the Cévennes was very strange.

STAGE 2

Le Monastier-sur-Gazeille to
Le Bouchet-St-Nicolas

Start	Le Monastier-sur-Gazeille
Finish	Le Bouchet-St-Nicolas
Distance	24km
Total ascent	785m
Total descent	495m
Time	6hr–6hr 30min
Refreshments	Supermarket, bakery, small cafés and restaurants in Le Monastier-sur-Gazeille; small café/bakery in St-Martin-de-Fugères mid-stage; small café (by the bridge) and restaurant in Goudet; café in Ussel; restaurant and small village shop in Le Bouchet-St-Nicolas

Robert Louis Stevenson started his journey from Le Monastier-sur-Gazeille, so this is the first day when the trail follows in his footsteps. Despite the length of this stage, it is a relatively easy day's walk. However, if you want to give yourself a slower, more relaxed start, you can split the stage and stay a night in Goudet (where there is a hotel, a *gîte* and a campsite), then continue to Le Bouchet-St-Nicolas the following day. This would obviously add a day to your trip but if you opt to divide this section in two and walk from Goudet to Le Bouchet-St-Nicolas, you can visit Lake Bouchet from the village. It is a great picnic spot and the trail around the lake makes for a pleasant afternoon stroll.

Start from the memorial plaque opposite the church near the pharmacy in **Le Monastier-sur-Gazeille**. With the memorial plaque on your right, follow place François d'Estaing. In the car park near the post office there is another memorial plaque, this one marking the place from which Stevenson and Modestine departed. Head steeply downhill until you reach rue Henri Debard, by the Église St Jean. Go right and descend with views of the valley, passing a caravan site on the left and a nursing home on the right.

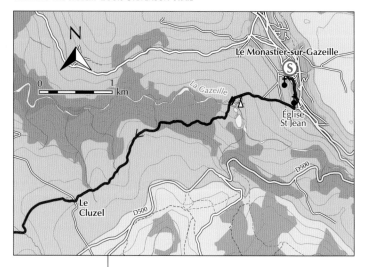

Follow the tarmac road downhill and, at the road junction, carry straight on. Keep going downhill, following the signs and ignoring any roads that join from the right. You'll pass a campsite and *gîte* on the left. Cross the bridge over the **Gazeille**, passing a hotel/restaurant on the riverbank just after the bridge. Ascend on the signposted forest track, ignoring any joining tracks.

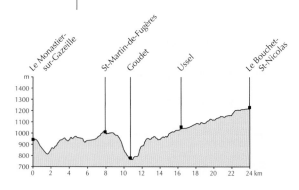

A small stream crosses the path and, when the forest track forks, carry straight on uphill as the red and white sign indicates.

Ignore the grassy path joining from the left and stay on the stony path. There is a meadow and views open up towards the hills. Pass a farm building on the left and some houses on the hillside. When the track splits, follow the sign right, downhill. Soon you ascend again, alongside a field. At a junction, go right, uphill on the well-trodden track. This track becomes an asphalt road by the first house in the hamlet of **Le Cluzel**. You will arrive at Le Cluzel about an hour after leaving Le Monastier-sur-Gazeille. Follow the signs between the houses, passing a trough and a shrine. At a road junction, follow the

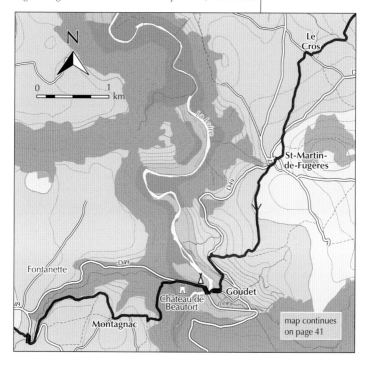

map continues
on page 41

Notice the old trail sign by the gîte.

sign straight on and pass a *gîte d'étape*. ◄ After the *gîte*, the tarmac road becomes a path again. On reaching a dirt track, keep left (as the GR70 sign indicates). Views of the hills fill the horizon as you walk past fields. A steep downhill section is followed by an ascent.

You will arrive at **Le Cros** hamlet about 15–20min after leaving Le Cluzel. At the junction, go right, downhill and, a few metres later, turn left off the tarmac road by a trough. When you reach the asphalt road again, turn right. At the junction, follow the sign left by the playground and picnic tables. The tarmac road becomes a dirt track and heads towards the hills. When you emerge onto an asphalt road (**D49**), go right, with views to the hills. Just before reaching the sign for St-Martin-de-Fugères, turn left off the D49. Follow this path through some fields, carrying straight on at a minor junction and, a few minutes later, arrive back at the asphalt road by a house. You will arrive in **St-Martin-de-Fugères** about 20–30min after leaving Le Cluzel. Pass a small World War 1 memorial, bear right, then go left by the church and continue downhill.

Walker descending towards Goudet on the stony path

At the minor junction, carry straight on. Follow the tarmac road between some stone houses and, just before

leaving St-Martin-de-Fugères, follow the sign left onto a dirt track. When the track splits, go left again (as the sign indicates). Enjoy the views of the hills. Soon you will descend among pine trees; pass a house and, just after, go right, downhill. Descend on a stony path, first through fields and then pine trees, and soon you will enjoy the views towards the River Loire and a château perched on the hill. Emerge onto the D49, cross over and continue on the other side as the red and white sign indicates. As you descend, more and more great views open up towards Goudet. You will arrive in **Goudet** near a small wooden plaque about Stevenson (1878–2018); follow the signs between the stone houses, ignoring any side roads. On reaching Le Bourg street, turn right, passing the Hôtel de la Loire and crossing a small bridge. Head towards the hill with the ruins of **Château de Beaufort** and cross the bridge over the **River Loire**. ▶

Château de Beaufort perched on the hill across the River Loire

Before you cross, the bank of the Loire near the bridge is a great place for a rest and a picnic.

The ruins of the **Château de Beaufort**, perched on the rocks overlooking the Loire, are prominent in Goudet. The château was built as a feudal castle in the 13th century. Later it was used for military

39

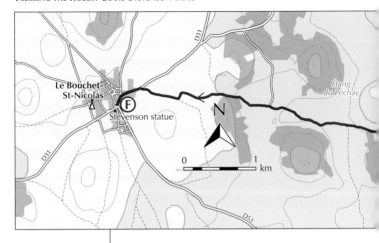

purposes and it played an important role during the Hundred Years War and the French Wars of Religion. It was abandoned after the 1789 Revolution. A new restoration project started in 2008 to save the château. If you want to visit the ruins, you need to arrange a time in advance: see www.chateaudebeaufort.fr/en.

Continue on the tarmac D49, leaving Goudet. About 10min later, you'll notice a clearing on the left-hand side of the road. There are trail signs by the road, and a path starts on the left. (If you have arranged in advance to visit the ruins of the castle, then take the path on the left of the clearing.) The trail continues slightly to the right of this clearing. Cross a stream over some rocks and continue uphill beneath the pine trees. On this steep uphill section, you might occasionally catch a glimpse of the castle overlooking the valley. The path then levels out for a while through the forest before it continues, slightly uphill, curving away from Goudet. At the junction (La Faye, alt 888m) carry straight on towards Ussel and enjoy the views of pine-covered hills on the left.

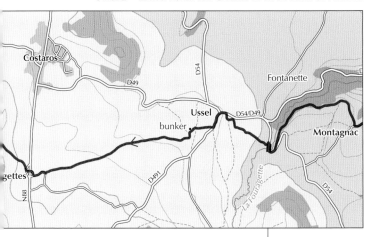

When you reach a surfaced road, go right and you will arrive at **Montagnac** about 30–40min after leaving Goudet. Walk through the village and, at the minor road junction, follow the sign to the right. The tarmac road becomes a path by the last house. There are views of the rolling hills on the right and then you start to ascend. When the path splits, continue straight on, slightly downhill. There is a gorge on the right and, on the other side, you can see the houses of Fontanette. When the grassy path splits, carry straight on. You can see the stream down below, and the sound of trickling water accompanies you as you walk between some blackberry bushes. Emerge onto a tarmac road (**D54**) by the trail signs. Go right, downhill, on this road. Cross the bridge over **La Fouragette** river, and leave the road to the left on a path a few metres after a house. A sign marks the path. Climb up above the house and then walk across a field, with views of the hills. Follow the track, which soon becomes an asphalt road by a house.

When you reach the main road (**D49**), go left. You will arrive at **Ussel** about 50min after leaving Montagnac. Follow the tarmac road through the village. ▸ At the road junction, bear left, as the sign indicates. Turn right

There is a small café (with donkey parking area) in the village.

41

towards Gîte Le Stevenson after the last house on the right. Pass Gîte Le Stevenson and the tarmac becomes a dirt track. At a small junction (La Chabanne, alt 1041m), go left as indicated on the 'Bargettes 2.4km' sign. Pass a **bunker**, and enjoy the views towards Costaros on the right. After the bunker at the dirt track junction, go left and, a few metres later at the next intersection (Les Martines, alt 1045m), turn right towards Bargettes. Ignore two joining tracks from the left and carry straight on.

At a junction, continue straight on and descend towards the houses of **Bargettes**, where the dirt track splits; continue straight on as the wooden GR70 sign indicates. ◄ At the tarmac road junction, go right and then immediately left. There is a wooden Stevenson sign. At Bargettes (alt 1092m) follow the trail signs straight on, towards 'Le Bouchet-St-Nicolas 5.1km'. Just before you reach the main **N88**, go right and follow this small tarmac road under the main road. On the other side of the road bear right, then immediately left by a house. Continue slightly uphill, past the last house and the tarmac road becomes a dirt track. When the track splits, bear left and then, a few metres later, join a gravel track (L'Étang du Péchay, alt 1128m) and continue straight on towards Le Bouchet-St-Nicolas. You have views towards the reservoir on the right.

At the junction with trail signs (Maar de Péchay, alt 1133m) go right ('St Nicolas 3.4km') and then immediately left as the red and white sign indicates. As you follow the grassy path, the scenery is dominated by fields and hills. When you reach a dirt track, turn right, and then go left at a junction, pass some farm buildings and you'll come to an asphalt road. Turn right and, a few metres later, leave the road to the left on a gravel road by a stone house. There is a sign indicating this. When the track splits, keep left. Notice an old wooden trail sign. Walk alongside fields and trees and soon the houses of **Le Bouchet-St-Nicolas** come into view. Follow the grassy path towards the buildings. When it splits, go right on a slightly overgrown path and then follow the signs on

There are some handwritten Robert Louis Stevenson quotes along the trail, and the first house might offer some refreshments.

a dirt track. When you reach another dirt track, go right towards the village.

On reaching the road (**D31**), go left. There is a wooden **statue** to commemorate Stevenson's visit.

L'Arrestadou (*chambres d'hôtes, gîte d'étape, table d'hôtes*), Route de Cayres, **www.larrestadou.fr**, tel +33 (0)4 71 57 35 34

La Retirade (*gîte d'étape, table d'hôtes*), Place de l'Église, **www.gitelaretirade.com**, contact@gitelaretirade.com, tel +33 (0)6 29 42 61 50

STEVENSON AND MODESTINE

Stevenson and Modestine started their journey together from Le Monastier-sur-Gazeille on Sunday 22 September 1878, and had hardly left the village when Stevenson experienced some difficulties. Modestine was so frustratingly slow that Stevenson started to wonder if they would ever make it to Alès. They came across a man who gave the writer some advice on how to handle his donkey, and the pair somehow made it to Goudet, where Stevenson stopped for lunch and sketched the Château de Beaufort.

On the climb from Goudet, Stevenson really struggled with Modestine. He also experienced some problems with his load, which finally toppled off Modestine's back in Ussel. No one helped Stevenson, and when he dragged the unwilling donkey through the village, the sight of them provided great entertainment to a group of locals. Grumpily, Stevenson left the village and then stopped to re-pack his bag. To lighten the load, he threw some of his stuff away, including the egg whisk. He wanted to camp by the Lac du Bouchet, but he got lost and never made it to the lake. He spent the night at an inn in Le Bouchet-St-Nicolas.

STAGE 3
Le Bouchet-St-Nicolas to Langogne

Start	Le Bouchet-St-Nicolas
Finish	Langogne
Distance	28.5km
Total ascent	395m
Total descent	690m
Time	7hr 30min
Refreshments	Small shop in Le Bouchet-St-Nicolas; bakery, shop and cafés in Landos and in Pradelles; shops, bakeries, cafés and restaurants in Langogne

This might be a long section but the terrain is not demanding. Follow the well-signposted dirt tracks between Le Bouchet-St-Nicolas and Landos. Then walk alongside fields, and stroll between the old stone buildings of Pradelles before arriving at Langogne. To shorten your day, you could finish this section in Pradelles, which is considered to be one of the prettiest villages in France.

In **Le Bouchet-St-Nicolas**, face the wooden Stevenson statue and go left. Leaving the houses behind, the tarmac road becomes a dirt track and, when it splits, take the left branch. There might be other tracks joining from either side, but the route is well signposted. ◀ At the dirt track junction, carry straight on and a few minutes later ignore a track on the left. Shortly after, when the dirt track splits, keep left. Leave the dirt track on a grassy path to the right, and the houses of Landos houses come into view. Ignore a dirt track on the right and another one just before a house. Pass the house and, just after the building, leave the dirt track to the right on a grassy path; there is a wooden Stevenson sign there. Walk slightly downhill alongside fields. Cross a stream on a wooden bridge and then continue slightly uphill on a narrow path. About 1hr 20min after leaving Le Bouchet-St-Nicolas, emerge onto

Hills fill the horizon as you walk alongside fields.

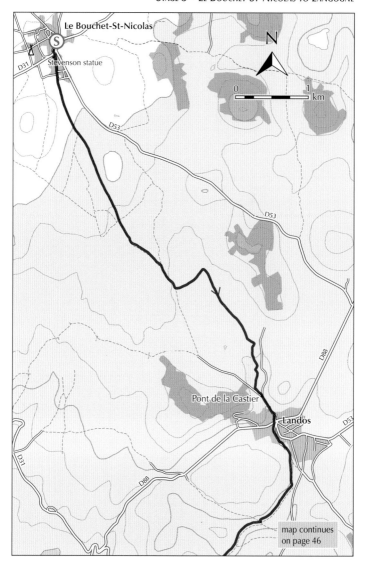

map continues
on page 46

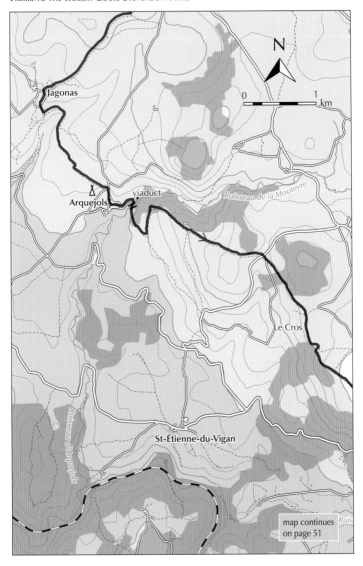

map continues on page 51

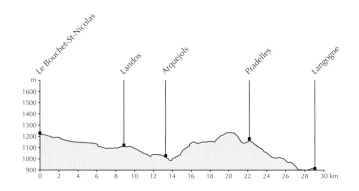

a tarmac road by trail signs and go left. Join another tarmac road near an old stone bridge (**Pont de La Castier**) and turn right.

On reaching **Landos** pass the village laundry and fountain. Go right by the trough, as the 'Pradelles 14.5km' sign indicates. At the junction with the Hôtel de Ville, cross the road and continue on rue de Coin, following the signs. Carry straight on by the next fountain (a dirt track goes to the right). Walk alongside fields and, when the dirt track splits, keep right (there are some houses on the left). Emerge onto another dirt track by a cross and go right, parallel to the railway. The houses of Landos nestle on the right and there is a farm on the other side of the railway on the left as you continue on the dirt track. At the junction go left; the track immediately splits into three: turn sharp right uphill. At the next junction, continue straight on. Hills dominate the views on the left. Go right at the dirt track junction. The track soon becomes surfaced road, follow it towards the buildings of the hamlet of Jagonas. When the road splits, go left (there is a trough on the right). Walk through **Jagonas** (about 1hr after Landos), past some houses and barns and, at the small road junction, go left and follow the tarmac road. At the three-way junction (Jagonas, alt 1041m) take the

Crops, fields and hills dominate the scenery with mountains in the background.

first left on the gravel road. At the next intersection, go right on a dirt track and, when it splits, keep left. ◀

The dirt track becomes tarmac again by a small **campsite** and you descend towards the houses of Arquejols. At the T-junction go left and a few metres later turn right, arriving in **Arquejols** about 30min after Jagonas. When the road splits, go right (there are picnic tables here). At the next intersection (Arquejols, alt 1004m) head left, downhill; you'll see a stream in the valley below on the right. The **viaduct** over the valley comes into view as you continue downhill. Cross a bridge over the stream – **Ruisseau de la Mouteyre** – and the tarmac road becomes dirt track again. Continue uphill with views towards more fields and mountains. Walk under the disused railway and then go left after the tunnel. Shortly after, the dirt track steers away from the railway. ◀ Follow the dirt track and, when its splits, carry straight on. When you reach a narrow tarmac road, cross over and continue straight on towards a group of pine trees. You can spot the Lac de Naussac reservoir in the distance to the south. Follow the tarmac road for about 150m towards Le Cros and then

There are some pine trees on the hillside and if you look back you can see the viaduct with the railway and some great views of the mountains.

When you leave Arquejols, meadows and rolling hills dominate the views near the disused railway

turn left onto a dirt track and head towards pine trees (there's a farm on the right on the hillside). At the next junction continue straight on beside fields, with views towards the reservoir.

There are some electricity poles near the track and, when you join another dirt track, go right and immediately take the path on the left uphill as indicated on the sign. A few minutes later you join a dirt track and follow the sign to the right. There are more views towards the reservoir. Pine trees and different shrubs populate this area, and soon the houses of Pradelles come into sight. Walk past a track with a barrier on the right and carry straight on. At the junction (**La Fagette**), go right downhill as the 'Pradelles 2.1km' sign indicates. At the intersection continue straight on (ignoring the tracks with barriers).

Descend towards Pradelles – you can also see Langogne in the distance. Emerge onto the tarmac road and turn left; almost immediately leave this road to the right, as the sign indicates. Firstly, walk parallel to the main road, and then go left on rue Robert Louis Stevenson. On arriving at **Pradelles** (about 2hr–2hr 30min from Arquejol) you will emerge onto the **D40** and turn right. ▶ Follow the signs through Pradelles. At the road junction, cross the main road and continue straight on and then go right by the fountain. Join the main road, keep left and pass the old fountain. Cross the road and head towards the tourist office, past the war memorial and past another fountain. Old stone houses line the street. Leave the old town via the town gate (Portail du Besset). Descend past old buildings and another fountain and carry straight on. After the Chapelle Notre-Dame de Pradelles, continue towards the cemetery. At the end of the cemetery car park continue straight on along the dirt track. There is a small vegetable garden on the left; carry straight on.

Cross a tarmac road and continue straight ahead, passing a barn and then ignoring a track on the left. When the dirt track splits, go right, downhill. Ignore a dirt track on the left. ▶ At the junction take the middle track. There is a farm on the hillside to the right. Ignore

In Pradelles you'll find a shop, bar, bakery, café and tourist office.

If you look back you can see Pradelles on the hillside.

The route goes between the old stone houses of Pradelles

There is an information board with a quote from Stevenson on a toilet building.

sidetracks as you walk slightly downhill; before long Langogne comes into full view. Pass a farmhouse then when you emerge onto a tarmac road, go left and continue downhill, enjoying the views of Langogne. When the road splits, keep left. On reaching another road, go left and cross the bridge over the **Ruisseau de la Ribeyre** and then go right along the **N88**. ◄ Keep right and cross a bridge over the **River Allier**, just like Robert Louis Stevenson did, and arrive at Langogne about 1hr after leaving Pradelles. After the bridge there is a supermarket where you can get some supplies. From the supermarket car park, go through a gate next to a hotel building, and

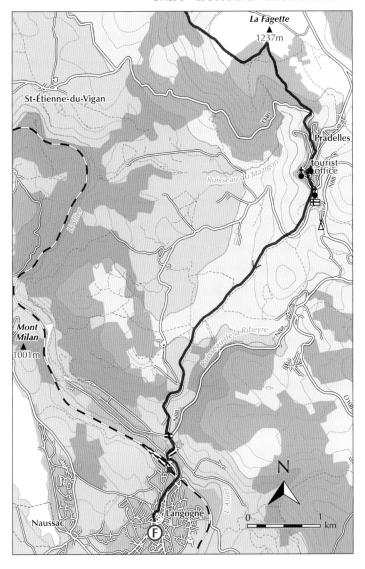

the trail continues alongside the river. Pass a picnic area and an open-air gym.

Emerge onto a tarmac road and continue straight on rue du Moulin de Sicard. Arriving back on the **N88**, cross the road and go immediately right uphill on rue de la Honde. Turn right uphill after Modest'inn, then turn left on rue Félix Viallet; at the junction you will see the tourist office. Keeping slightly right, follow the road to the old market square in the centre of **Langogne**.

The Romanesque church in **Langogne** dates back to the 12th century and the covered market in the town centre – the start of Stage 4 – was built in 1743.

Hôtel du Languedoc, 6 avenue du Maréchal Joffre, **www.hoteldulanguedoc-langogne.com**, hoteldu-languedoc.langogne@gmail.com, tel +33 (0)4 66 46 31 08

Modest'inn (*chambres d'hôtes, table d'hôtes*), 2 rue de la Honde, **www.modestinn-chambres-dhotes.fr**, modestinn.48@gmail.com, tel +33 (0)4 66 46 48 33

STEVENSON AND MODESTINE

Stevenson wanted to camp by the Lac du Bouchet but he couldn't find the lake before dusk, so he spent the night at the inn in Le Bouchet-St-Nicolas. He had to share the room with a young family, which he found a bit odd. In the morning he was given a stick with a pin at the end by the landlord. With this new – and painful – way of encouraging Modestine to walk, the pair reached Pradelles and then continued on to Langogne without any problems. Today walkers – just like Robert Louis Stevenson – arrive at Langogne by crossing the bridge over the River Allier.

STAGE 4
Langogne to Cheylard-l'Évêque

Start	Langogne
Finish	Cheylard-l'Évêque
Distance	16.5km
Total ascent	445m
Total descent	235m
Time	4hr
Refreshments	Cafés, restaurants, shops and bakeries in Langogne; make sure that you get the essentials here, as there are no shops until you get to La Bastide-Puylaurent, at the end of Stage 5

This is a short section so you can spend some time looking around and buying supplies in Langogne before setting off. Robert Louis Stevenson got desperately lost near Fouzilhac, but today the route shouldn't cause any trouble for walkers. You make your way alongside fields and then through forest and, after Fouzilhac, you descend to Cheylard-l'Évêque.

Between 1764 and 1767 a fierce animal terrorised the people of southern France, near Langogne. The **Beast of Gévaudan** was believed to be a wolf or a wolf-dog hybrid that killed mainly women and children. Hunters set out to track down the beast and its death was announced several times before the attacks finally stopped. Today it is believed that the beast might have been a sub-adult male lion. Although lions were known in France at the time, most people had never come across a wild one, therefore witnesses and survivors described the attacker as a 'beast'.

With your back towards the old covered marketplace in **Langogne**, go left on boulevard de Gaulle and then go right on rue du Pont Vieux. Cross the stone bridge (there

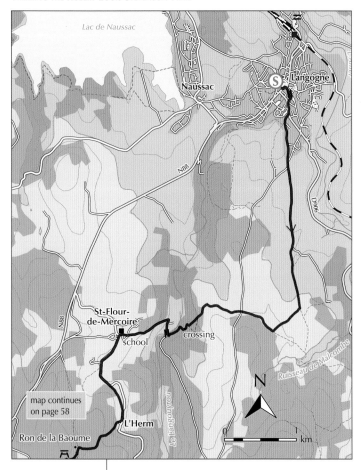

are GR70, 470 and 700 signs here) and, follow the sign to
the right. When you arrive at avenue du Maréchal Joffre
(D906), go left, past the 'Square Stevenson', which has a
picnic bench. After the picnic area the road splits: take
rue du 11 Novembre 1918 on the right. Ignoring any
side roads follow this road. Carry straight on after the last

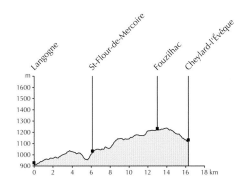

house and, at the junction with signs, keep left towards Brugerolles Les Chevailloux. Follow the tarmac road alongside fields with some views towards the mountains and wind turbines on the left.

About 30–40min from the old market square in Langogne, leave the tarmac road and turn right onto a dirt track. Ignoring a track on the left, pass a house and, a few minutes later at the junction, go right as the 'Cheylard 14km' sign indicates. Fields and pine trees dominate the landscape. At the T-junction go right slightly downhill with views to the mountains. The track soon evens out. When you reach a junction, carry straight on, downhill along the tarmac road towards some houses. On reaching the first house, go left on the grass and descend on the path alongside the fence and soon you will be walking through a forest. Go through a gate and continue downhill. This is private land, but trekkers are welcome (as the sign indicates). Descend through the forest, ignoring any side paths. Signs mark the well-trodden path. Cross a stream and then go through a gate, leaving the private land. Ignore a path on the left and continue slightly uphill. At the junction, keep right downhill. There is a trickling stream on your right as you follow the forest path. Cross a stone bridge over **Le Langouyrou** and walk up the tarmac road to reach **St-Flour-de-Mercoire**.

Follow the road uphill with some views towards the hills. Pass some houses and, a few minutes later, you will arrive at a junction with the old laundry building, school, bus stop and World War 1 memorial. Go left with the laundry building and trough on your right. Follow the road (D71) through the village and after the village turn right onto a track. Notice a metal cross by the track and soon you will arrive back on a tarmac road. Go right and arrive at **L'Herm**. Pass a picnic bench and, at the road junction, turn right by the trough. ◀

La Tartine de Modestine café is signposted to the left but the trail continues to the right.

Follow the narrow tarmac road, which soon becomes a dirt track. At the track junction carry straight on and, at the intersection, join the forest path on the other side of the track. ◀ Ron de la Baoume (a huge boulder) is on the right. Joining another path from the left, carry straight on and pass a **picnic area** (it is a great place to stop for a rest and picnic). At the junction by the picnic area take the middle path and walk through a clearing; shortly after you will be walking through forest again. Ignore a track on the left. Pass a small old stone house on the right. Cross a stream over a bridge, then emerge onto a tarmac road, go left and through **Sagnerousse**.

The forest floor is scattered with moss-covered rocks.

Walk through a clearing before returning to the forest near Sagnerousse

An information board about Robert Louis Stevenson's journey in the area explains an interesting theory, according to which the **magnetic field** in this area is disturbed as a result of faults and underground streams. This might explain why Stevenson was so desperately lost and experienced such difficulties finding his way in this area.

After the last house, leave the tarmac road and follow the sign to the right. Continue on a wide path alongside some fields. Go through a gated area and then walk among pine trees. A small stream goes under the path and then you start to ascend. ▶ About 30min from Sagnerousse you reach Fouzilhac. Turn left onto a tarmac road and continue to **Fouzilhic**, which is only about 300m away.

After Fouzilhic the tarmac becomes dirt track again, and fields and mountains dominate the scenery. At the next junction go left as the GR70 sign indicates. (From this junction, if you carry straight on, Hôtel de France in Chaudeyrac is about 2km away. It is signposted. It can be an alternative place to stay if you can't find

Just before Fouzilhac there are great views towards the mountains.

Looking back towards Fouzilhic

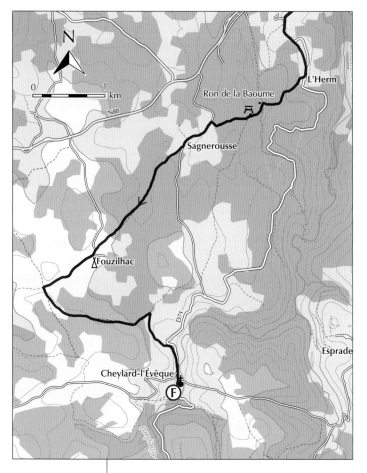

accommodation in the small Cheylard-l'Évêque. Bear in mind that this detour would add 5km to the next stage.)

Walk through the forest and, at the next intersection, go left, downhill. At the junction, go right, as the 'Cheylard 1km' sign indicates, and enjoy some views towards the hills. Ignore a track on the right and carry straight on. Descend to the valley and soon the houses of Cheylard-l'Évêque come into view. Emerge onto a tarmac road (**D71**) by the **Cheylard-l'Évêque** sign, turn right and walk into the village.

> In **Cheylard-l'Évêque** you can see the Chapelle Notre-Dame-de-Toutes-Graces (Our Lady of all Graces) perched on the hill on the right overlooking the village, and there is a stream on the left. There is a small café/bar in the village but don't rely on it as its opening times may be irregular.

Le Refuge du Moure (*chambres d'hôtes, gîte d'étape, table d'hôtes*), **www.lozere-gite.com**, info@lozere-gite.com, tel +33 (0)4 66 69 03 21

Alternatively, you can stay in Hôtel de France in Chaudeyrac, **www.hoteldefrance-lozere.com**, info@hoteldefrance-lozere.com, tel +33 (0)4 66 47 91 00

STEVENSON AND MODESTINE

Stevenson spent the whole morning writing his journal and only left Langogne at 2pm. He was planning to walk to Cheylard-l'Évêque, but there was no clear direct route and he got hopelessly lost. Nightfall was approaching and he was desperately trying to make it to Cheylard-l'Évêque. He stumbled upon the tiny hamlet of Fouzilhic and asked for guidance, but then he lost his way again and came across another hamlet, Fouzilhac, in the dark. He knocked on doors but the residents refused to give him any help. Stevenson sensed that the locals were scared to leave their houses after nightfall in fear of the infamous Beast of Gévaudan.

The frustrated Robert Louis Stevenson had little choice but to camp in the dark near the hamlet. Much to his surprise he slept quite well, in spite of the damp weather.

They set off in the morning and came upon Fouzilhic again, where he met the man who had tried to direct him towards Cheylard-l'Évêque the previous night. The old man was horrified to learn that Stevenson had spent the night in the woods and he walked with the writer until the houses of Cheylard-l'Évêque came into sight.

STAGE 5
Cheylard-l'Évêque to La Bastide-Puylaurent

Start	Cheylard-l'Évêque
Finish	La Bastide-Puylaurent
Distance	20km; 27km with detour to the monastery
Total ascent	410m; 675m with detour to the monastery
Total descent	500m; 770m with detour to the monastery
Time	5hr 30min; 7hr-7hr 30min with detour to monastery
Refreshments	None along the way. There is a café, restaurant and a small village shop in La Bastide-Puylaurent

Follow the well-signposted forest tracks from Cheylard-l'Évêque. The forest floor is home to many different kinds of mushroom, and you might meet people picking wild ingredients to prepare local dishes. You can wander among the ruins of the Château de Luc and enjoy some fine views towards the valley before arriving at Luc. An optional detour will take you along wide forest tracks to the Abbaye Notre Dame des Neiges.

Follow the red and white signs along the D71 through **Cheylard-l'Évêque**, crossing two bridges. After the Forestry Department office building – just before another

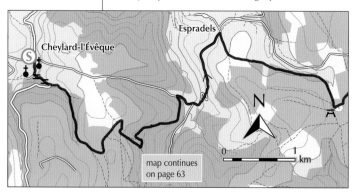

map continues on page 63

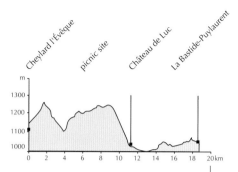

bridge at a bend in the road – turn left onto a track heading slightly uphill. There is a gorge with trickling water on the right. Ignore other tracks, first on the right and then on the left and carry straight on slightly uphill. When the forest track splits, keep left. At the T-junction go left and then at the next intersection turn right. Ignore a track on the right and carry straight on downhill. Follow the forest track as it turns back on itself and ignore any sidetracks. Views open up towards the mountains as you descend through forest and, about 1hr after leaving Cheylard-l'Évêque, you will come to a tarmac road where you turn right. Follow this road, cross a bridge – ignore one dirt track before and one after the bridge – and continue uphill on the single-lane tarmac road with great views.

Turn right off the tarmac road and head uphill on a stony track. A few minutes later, cross the tarmac road and continue uphill on the stony path through bushes. Shortly after, you will emerge onto a road, go left and follow it uphill with some mountain views. The hamlet of Espradels comes into sight on the hillside. Just before reaching **Espradels**, turn right onto a track. Pass a trough and about 300m later follow the sign left onto another track. There are fields by the trail and you have some mountain views. Descend for a while and soon you will join a stony track, where you bear right and then turn left onto a path, as the sign indicates. Shortly after you will pass a picnic area beneath trees by a pond. Keep left

The trail passes a pond about 45min before Château de Luc

with the pond on your right. Cross a wooden bridge and continue along the path.

On reaching a stony track, go left and, when it splits, take the right branch. Follow the stony track downhill on the hillside covered in pine trees. Carry straight on under the high-voltage cable and, joining a tarmac road, continue straight on again. Follow the road for about 500m and turn right onto a narrow path. Descend with some views, cross a narrow tarmac road and carry straight on. Follow the narrow forest path and soon you will cross the tarmac road again and continue downhill. You will rejoin the same tarmac road by a Stevenson information board about 45min after the pond. Cross the road and continue downhill then, just before reaching the ruins of **Château de Luc**, turn right, downhill. ◀

You might want to spend some time wandering among the ruins and enjoying the great views of the valley.

> **Château de Luc** was built during the 12th century and for 100 years it belonged to the Luc family. It held off a number of sieges during the Hundred Years War. However, by the time of the French Revolution the château was neglected. Later it was renovated and the white statue of the Madonna was

placed on the top in 1878. In his journal, Robert Louis Stevenson mentions the château's brand new statue.

Descend towards the houses of **Luc** and when you reach a tarmac road turn right. (To the left, the red and white signs take you through the village and then the marked route – to avoid walking about 800m on the D906 – makes a detour of almost 4km. You can also see the GR sign by the road, and the route described here

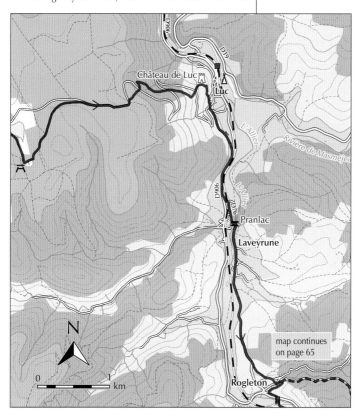

map continues on page 65

Church in Laveyrune

follows the old signs.) Join another tarmac road and go left towards the church. Pass the church and a war memorial and leave Luc by the cemetery. On reaching the **D906** near the railway, go right. A few minutes later at the road junction leave the D906 to the left along the D76 and arrive at **Pranlac**. Cross the railway and then turn right. Pass a trough. At the junction follow the sign left and, crossing the bridge, you will arrive at **Laveyrune**. Turn right after crossing the river. (You might see some confusing signs here.) Follow the road and at a junction carry straight on, pass a church and leave the hamlet. Walk up the road with views towards the mountains, go past a track on the left and carry straight on. Follow the red and white sign left onto a dirt track, then, at the junction, carry straight on as the 'La Bastide 3.6km' sign indicates. Descend on the stony track, cross a tarmac road and continue downhill. Cross a stream over a bridge and then carry on up the road.

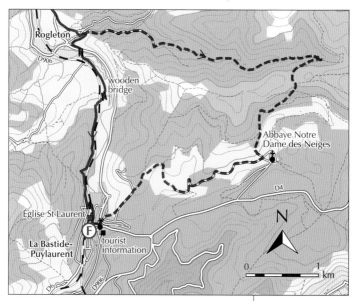

To La Bastide-Puylaurent without the detour to the monastery

Turn right off the tarmac road as the 'La Bastide' sign indicates (but continue straight on if you want to see the monastery). Pass the houses of **Rogleton** above and you will come to the **D906**. Continue on the other side of the road, cross an old bridge, and turn left off the D906 onto a dirt track. A railway line runs near the track. Climb the stile over the fence then cross a **wooden bridge**. Turn right slightly uphill, and then go under the railway. Walk up through the forest and at a junction turn left. Follow the shrub-lined path parallel to the railway. There are views of the hillside scattered with houses. When you come to a tarmac road, go left downhill. At the junction turn left towards the village. The next section of the GR70 continues to the right. Cross the railway and arrive at **La Bastide-Puylaurent** about 45min after you left the tarmac road in Rogleton.

There aren't many accommodation options to choose from in La Bastide-Puylaurent.

Hôtel La Grand Halt, rue des Tilleuls, www.hotel-lagrandhalte.fr, tel +33 (0)4 66 46 00 35

Hôtel Les Genêts, rue des Tilleuls, hotelgenets@hotmail.fr, tel +33 (0)4 66 46 00 13

To La Bastide-Puylaurent with the detour to the monastery

Some wide forest tracks will lead you to the Trappist monastery. The signs can be confusing in places and the distances given on the signs are not always correct. This detour adds an extra 7km to your day.

Continue along the tarmac road (ignoring the trail on the right signposted towards La Bastide-Puylaurent). Pass a dirt track on the right and continue on the road as indicated by the 'Monastery 5.2km' sign. Ignore two more dirt tracks on the left and continue straight on. A few minutes later the tarmac road becomes a forest track. When it splits, take the left branch and follow the forest track for about 30–40min then ignore a track on the left and carry straight on as the 'Notre Dame des Neiges 2.4km' sign indicates. Shortly after, at a junction, turn sharp right (as indicated on 'Notre Dame des Neiges 1.8km' sign). Follow the well-trodden forest track ignoring another track on the right. At a junction continue straight on downhill. A few minutes later at the next junction carry straight on and soon views open up to the east. The forest track becomes a sealed road, ignore a track on the right and you will come to the monastery of **Notre Dame des Neiges**.

The **Trappist monastery** of Notre Dame des Neiges (Our Lady of the Snows) was built it 1850 but was destroyed by a devastating fire in 1912. It was rebuilt, so the buildings you see today are not the ones Stevenson stayed in. It is possible to spend a night at the monastery, but you have to book ahead.

At a junction near the monastery turn right towards the old chapel, as indicated on the 'La Bastide 3km' sign. Notice the red and white signs as you follow the road past a building. Walk alongside fields and then some pine trees. At the junction go right uphill. Near a house turn left onto a dirt track.

At the next junction go left, pass a house and, at a T-junction, turn left as indicated on the 'La Bastide 1km' sign. Follow the red and white signs on the well-trodden forest track. Emerge onto a tarmac road, go left and, shortly after, the houses of **La Bastide-Puylaurent** appear in the valley. Turn right off the road onto a path, pass a house and then rejoin the tarmac road; go left and head towards the church.

For accommodation in La Bastide-Puylaurent, see above.

STEVENSON AND MODESTINE

Robert Louis Stevenson breakfasted and wrote his journal in the friendly inn in Cheylard-l'Évêque. He was not impressed with Cheylard or Luc and wondered why anyone would want to visit these places. He then quickly reassured himself with his most quoted thoughts: 'For my part, I travel not to go anywhere, but to go. I travel for travel's sake.' He spent a shivering cold night in a large, clean inn in Luc. The statue of Our Lady on the Château de Luc was brand new at the time of his visit. From Luc, Stevenson and Modestine continued by the river to La Bastide-Puylaurent and then, leaving the river, they carried on to the Trappist monastery of Our Lady of the Snows. Because of his views on religion, Stevenson was nervous about visiting the monastery; however, he spent a night there and described life in the monastery and the people he met there, including an Irishman who was eager to talk to Stevenson while he gave him a guided tour. Mostly the monks lived under a strict vow of silence. Their daily routine started at 2am and, from September until Easter they fasted, only eating one meal a day; the rest of the year they ate twice daily.

STAGE 6
La Bastide-Puylaurent to Le Bleymard

Start	La Bastide-Puylaurent
Finish	Le Bleymard
Distance	30km
Total ascent	900m
Total descent	850m
Time	7hr 30min–8hr
Refreshments	Village shop and café/bar/restaurant in La Bastide-Puylaurent; café in Chasseradès; supermarket and bakery in Le Bleymard

This is a long section but you will be rewarded with the wonderful mountainous scenery. From La Bastide-Puylaurent, firstly follow some well-signposted, wide dirt tracks and then you can admire the impressive Mirandol viaduct, before walking through forest and eventually descending to Le Bleymard. You can divide this stage into two shorter days by staying a night in Chasseradès.

From the church in **La Bastide-Puylaurent** – Église St Laurent – follow the road towards the railway station and cross a bridge. After the bridge turn right towards the station and cross the railway tracks. At the junction take the middle track uphill towards 'La Mourade 3.3km', as the GR70 sign indicates. Leaving the houses behind, the road becomes a dirt track and views open up to the mountains as you ascend. Ignore an asphalt road on the left, and soon you will be rewarded with fine views.

When you come to a junction, ignore the path on the right and continue on the wide, well-trodden track with views towards mountains on your left. Ignore any joining tracks. At **La Mourade** (alt 1300m), carry straight on. Pass some wind turbines, ignoring tracks on the right. When the track splits go right (there is a wind turbine on the left) and when you reach a junction, carry straight

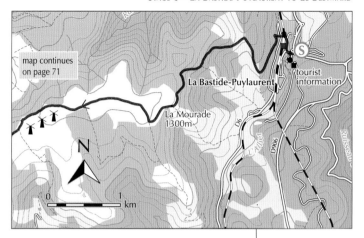

map continues on page 71

on. Descend among trees, passing a grassy path on the left. At a junction, Les Taillades (alt 1290m), turn left and, a few minutes later, at the next intersection go right. ▸

At the next intersection go left and, immediately after, ignore a track on the left. There are fine views to the forest-covered mountains. Descend, ignoring any joining tracks, and you will reach some houses about 2hr after leaving La Bastide-Puylaurent. ▸ At the junction, turn right downhill on the tarmac road and cross a

There are wind turbines on the left.

Notice a Stevenson scarecrow with a wooden Modestine that holds a GR70 sign.

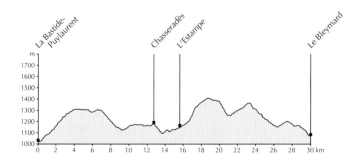

Views towards the
mountains near La
Bastide-Puylaurent

bridge. Turn right onto a dirt track, as the red and white
sign indicates. Cross a stream and follow the stony track
slightly uphill. Ignore a track on the right and continue
past a barn. The track becomes tarmac again by a building. At the junction go left, pass some houses and you
will come to the **D6**; go right. There is a *gîte* by the road.
At the junction stay on the main road, curving slightly to
the right. Ignore a road on the right and follow the D6
towards Mende. Mountains dominate the scenery on the
left and there is a hotel building by the road.

At the next junction go right to **Chasseradès**. Follow
the red and white signs through the village. Pass the
church and continue towards the **cemetery**. After the
cemetery, descend on the narrow tarmac road with
views of the mountains. Walk between houses and, as
you descend towards the valley, **Mirandol** with its viaduct comes into view. Pass a *gîte* and walk past more
houses and then under a small road bridge. Then turn
left and walk under the enormous viaduct. Follow the
signs through the village, and cross a bridge. After the
houses turn right onto a path heading uphill. The path
then curves left – ignore a track on the right. On reaching

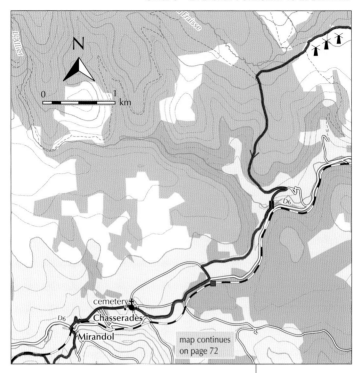

map continues
on page 72

a track, turn sharp right. You have views towards the mountains as you descend. After a short distance you will walk alongside the railway with a meadow on the left and with mountains dominating the scenery in front of you. At the junction with a stone cross, continue right downhill.

When you come to a tarmac road, go left and walk through the hamlet of **L'Estampe** and follow the **D120**. About 5–10min later, turn right off the winding tarmac road onto a dirt track. When the path splits, keep left on a stony path uphill through the forest. You will join a forest track and turn left and, a few minutes later, re-emerge onto the D120 tarmac road and go right. Follow

Wide open views of the landscape near the hamlet of L'Estampe

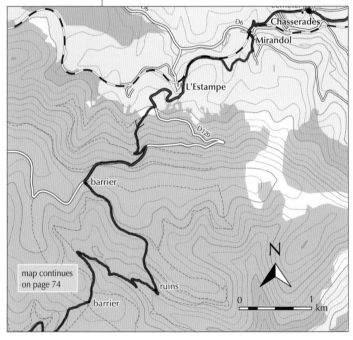

Chasserades

D6

Mirandol

L'Estampe

D120

barrier

map continues
on page 74

ruins

barrier

N

0   1
km

the road ignoring a track first on the left and then, shortly after, one on the right. Where two tracks leave the tarmac road to the left, take the second track, as indicated. Pass a **barrier** and then descend along a forest track, ignoring a grassy track on the right and then one on the left. When the track splits, keep right, slightly downhill, ignoring any joining tracks. ▸

As you descend rustling leaves and bird song will entertain you.

At the junction go right, as indicated on the 'Le Bleymard 8.5km' sign, and pass the **ruins** of some abandoned stone buildings. After the ruins the path splits, keep left (the other path is overgrown) downhill through thick forest. you will pass a streambed on the right. At the junction, go right on the stony path curving uphill. Ignore a track on the left and continue on the well-trodden path. When you get to the hairpin bend, take a sharp left-hand turn uphill, ignoring a path on the right. A forest track joins from the right; carry straight on ignoring a track on the left. Emerge onto a dirt track by the **barrier** – about 1hr after leaving the D120 – turn right and immediately leave the dirt track on a path to the left, heading downhill through a forest. Descend steeply with some great views. At a T-junction, go right and, at the next intersection with signs, carry straight on. Descend along the narrow path, with a stream on your right. Join a forest path and go right. Cross the stream and then emerge onto a forest track and go right again. Whe you get to a junction, carry straight on.

A little over an hour after the second barrier, you will reach a tarmac road; go left, and you will be greeted with fine mountain views (there is a *gîte* on the right on the hillside). Descend towards the houses and then follow the signs through **Les Alpiers**. Pass a *gîte* and, soon after, the tarmac road becomes a dirt track. When it splits, keep left and descend on a stony path with views towards **Le Bleymard**. You will arrive at the tarmac road (**D901**) about 30min after Les Alpiers; there is a campsite to the left, or you turn right to the village.

La Remise (hotel), **www.hotel-laremise.com**, contact@hotel-laremise.com, tel +33 (0)4 66 48 65 80

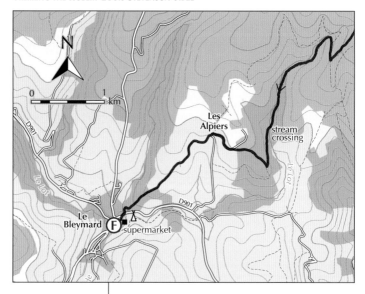

La Combette (*chambres d'hôtes, table d'hôtes*),
www.lacombette.com, lacombette@hotmail.fr, tel +33
(0)6 86 34 01 86

STEVENSON AND MODESTINE

Leaving late from the monastery, Stevenson and Modestine followed the
Allier river and reached Chasseradès at sundown. They spent the night at
an inn, where Stevenson discussed politics well into the night with five men
who were surveying for the new railway.

On the following day (28 September) Stevenson left the inn early and
descended to the valley of Chassezac. They walked across the tiny Lestampes
(L'Estampe), where Stevenson was amazed to see so many sheep. He then
zigzagged uphill, much to Modestine's annoyance; otherwise he seemed to
have less trouble with his four-legged companion, or maybe he had started
to focus on different things. Stevenson entered the Cévennes contented and
looking forward to the rest of his journey. He had dinner in Le Bleymard and
then left the village and camped among pine trees.

STAGE 7
Le Bleymard to Le Pont-de-Montvert

Start	Le Bleymard
Finish	Le Pont-de-Montvert
Distance	21km
Total ascent	670m
Total descent	820m
Time	6hr
Refreshments	Supermarket and bakeries in Le Bleymard; café/bar at Mont Lozère ski station (open year-round); cafés and restaurants, bakery and grocery shop in Le Pont-de-Montvert

This is one of the most picturesque sections of the trail. A steep climb from Le Bleymard will be rewarded with some fine views. You reach the highest part of the trail, the Pic de Finiels, and then descend to Le Pont-de-Monvert with some more fantastic views. It is easy to see why Stevenson was taken by the landscape.

Follow the **D901** through **Le Bleymard**. Take the first left after the supermarket, opposite La Remise hotel (route du Mont Lozère) towards La Mairie (town hall), over the river. Then take the middle lane by the statue of doctor and anatomist Henri Rouvière. Follow the signs between houses and look out for the church on the left. Go left on Place de l'Église as the GR70 sign indicates. Pass the war memorial and church and follow the curving road by the Mairie, then turn right steeply uphill. Turn right off the road onto a dirt track, as the red and white sign indicates. When the dirt track splits, carry straight on on the stony path, above some houses with extensive views.

Pine-covered mountains dominate the scenery as you leave the village behind. Walk along the edge of the forest, then turn right onto a dirt track, and enjoy the great scenery. At the five-way junction, **Col Santel**, carry

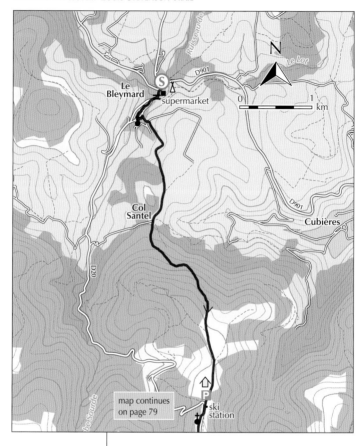

straight on uphill (the GR44 and GR68 peel off and the GR7 and GR70 run together uphill). The forest track levels out for a while, but soon you will ascend again. When the track splits, take the right branch steeply uphill. At a clearing ignore a track joining from the right and carry straight on. You then walk alongside a fence with views to Mont Lozère and soon the buildings of the ski station come into view.

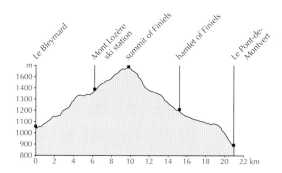

▶ When a dirt track joins from the left, carry straight on. Follow the wide ridge and, about 1hr 20min after leaving Le Bleymard, you will arrive at the car park of the **Mont Lozère ski station**. Near the ticket office, keep left parallel to the D20. Cross the **D20** (the GR7 continues to the left) and the GR70 trail continues past a modern chapel. Ascend with the ski lift cable in sight, cross a dirt track near an antenna, and carry straight on. ▶ Shortly after, standing stones mark the path as you continue uphill with extensive views; Finiels is teasingly visible. About 50min after leaving the ski station, you arrive at a junction and take the path on the right leading to the summit. (The left path goes down to the hamlet of Finiels;

The views are dominated by bare mountains, covered only with some shrubs and grass.

Pine trees and bilberry bushes (*Vaccinium myrtillus*) populate the mountainside.

Outstanding views from Mount Lozére

The hamlet of Finiels

in bad weather it is advisable to avoid the summit and take this path to the hamlet). About 15–20min later you will reach the summit of Finiels (alt 1699m), the highest point of the GR70 trail.

Enjoy the fine panoramic views and then go west downhill on a grassy path. Soon you will notice some waymarks on rocks. Descend with excellent views until you reach a path and turn left between pine trees. Leave this path to the right, following the sign downhill. Keep left when the path splits and continue the descent. Follow the narrow stony path through pine forest. When you arrive at a forest track, go right and almost immediately join another track and turn left. Pass a stone shelter. As you follow the forest track, you might pass some bee-hives near the track. A dirt track joins from the right; carry straight on. When the track splits, go right, and at the next junction go left downhill alongside fields with some more great mountain views. At the next intersection, bear left downhill. The stony track becomes a surfaced road. When you get to the tarmac road (D20), turn right downhill towards the houses and arrive at the hamlet of **Finiels**

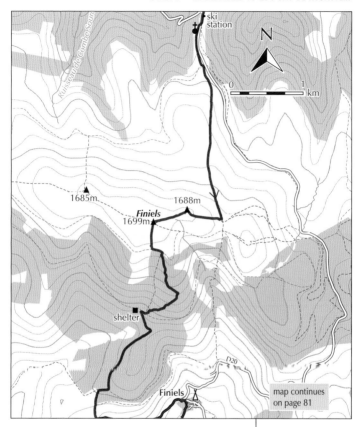

about 1hr 30min after leaving the summit. There is a *gîte* and campsite here.

Take the first turn on the right and pass the fountain (drinking water). At a junction go right, pass a small cemetery and walk alongside vegetable gardens. The tarmac road becomes a dirt track and, when it splits, go left as the red and white sign indicates. The views are dominated by rock-scattered hillsides. A stream runs near the track. When the track splits, carry straight on; there are

As you descend on the stony path, there are some great views to the valley and the houses of Le Pont-de-Montvert.

some houses on the left. Turn right then cross a road and carry straight on. Pass some houses, then bear left on a grassy path through fields with a couple of gates. Cross a small stream and go through more gates, and then turn left, downhill. ◀ You will pass the remains of an old terraced cultivated area on the right.

Cross a small stream, pass a house and follow the stony path downhill. Shortly after, descend alongside a drystone wall towards the village and pass a deep ravine on the left. Arrive at a tarmac road by a house, ignore the path on the right and go through a gated area. Follow the signs to the village centre. Join the tarmac road and follow it downhill. When you get to another tarmac road, go left and cross the bridge. Arrive at **Le Pont-de-Montvert** about 2hr after the hamlet of Finiels.

A narrow path leading to Le Pont-de-Montvert

Le Pont-de-Montvert was a local centre of **Protestants** (Huguenots) in the 17th century. The Edict of Nantes, signed by Henry IV of France in 1598, granted the Protestants in France the right to practice their religion. However, the edict was revoked by Louis XIV in 1685 and, as a result,

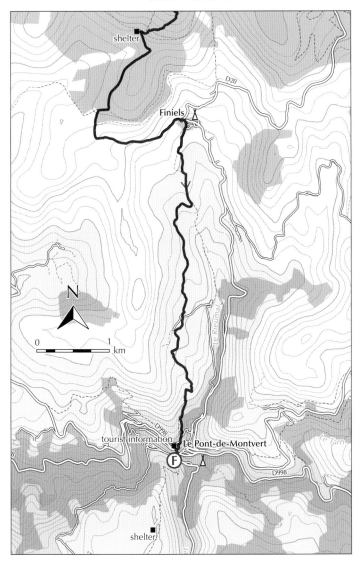

Le Pont-de-Montvert and the River Tarn

Protestant schools were closed and churches were destroyed. Many Protestants fled France. François Langdale, the French Catholic Abbé of Chaila, used his house in Le Pont-de-Montvert as a prison where he tortured Protestants. On 24 July 1702 Langdale was murdered, marking the beginning of the War of the Camisards, the Protestant peasants' uprising in the Cévennes against royal authority.

Gîtes du Chastel, Quartier de la Moline, **www.cevennes-gites.com**, gitesduchastel@cevennes-gites.com, tel +33 (0)6 80 21 14 10

Auberges des Cévennes, **www.auberge-des-cevennes.com**, lescevennes@orange.fr, tel +33 (0)4 66 45 80 01

STEVENSON AND MODESTINE

Stevenson was quickly taken by the wild landscape and he truly enjoyed the night that he spent in the woods near Le Bleymard. There was a hint in his account that he missed a female companion and would have liked to share the experience with someone special. He was so satisfied with his 'bed' in the woods that he left some money in the turf to pay for the night. He admired the views from the peak of Finiels and then quickly descended. Stevenson stopped in Le Pont-de-Montvert to eat and write his journal. He was excited about entering the Cévennes and was looking forward to the journey ahead. He was also interested in the history of the Camisards in the area.

He left Le Pont-de-Montvert admiring the views and didn't cover a great distance before sunset, so he camped beneath chestnut trees.

STAGE 8
Le Pont-de-Montvert to Florac

Start	Le Pont-de-Montvert
Finish	Florac
Distance	30km
Total ascent	820m
Total descent	1180m
Time	7hr 30min–8hr
Refreshments	Bakery, small shop, cafés and restaurants in Le Pont-de-Montvert; supermarket, bakeries, cafés and restaurants in Florac

From Le Pont-de-Montvert Stevenson followed a road by the Tarn; today the GR70 trail deviates from his route and takes you over the mountains. From Le Pont-de-Montvert climb on a narrow path and, looking back, you can enjoy some wonderful views of the stone houses clinging to the banks of Tarn. It is a long and demanding section, but grand views accompany you most of the day.

From the tourist information office in **Le Pont-de-Montvert**, cross the bridge and keep left; then go right on the first narrow street, opposite the Auberge des Cévennes. Soon you zigzag uphill, on the well-trodden path, ignoring a small path on the right. ◄ The scenery is dominated by rock-scattered mountainsides and soon you will pass a deep valley on the left. About 40–45min after leaving Le Pont-de-Montvert, you will pass a small stone shelter with some excellent views all around.

You can enjoy the fantastic bird's-eye views of Le Pont-de-Montvert in the valley.

From the shelter the path levels out for a while and there is a fence on either side of the path. Join a track, go left and soon after you will pass a track on the right and, further on, an enclosure. Descend slightly and, when you come to a dirt track junction, go left through a gate. Continue downhill on the narrow path with great views towards pine-covered mountains. Go through another

gate, and soon you will be walking through beech forest. The forest floor is cluttered with moss-covered rocks and you will pass a small stream on your left, which might be dry. Ignore a path on the left and stay on the well-trodden path. Cross the stream(bed) on rocks. When you reach a tarmac road about 45min after the stone shelter, go left

Rock-scattered plateau near Le Pont-de-Montvert

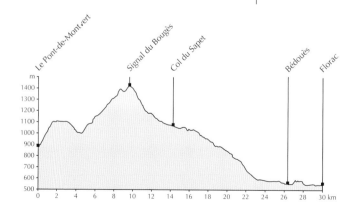

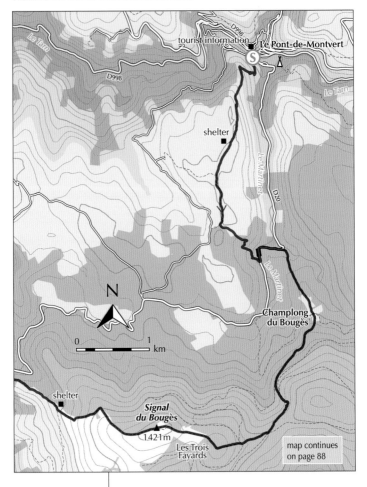

map continues on page 88

and cross a small bridge over **Le Martinet**. About 500m later leave this tarmac road to the right uphill on a dirt track. It becomes surfaced road and runs through forest, and then changes back to a stony track. It is a long uphill haul.

Pass **Champlong du Bougès** *gîte* and a small reservoir. At the junction continue straight on uphill as the 'Florac 23km' sign indicates. It is a steep climb but the track levels out for a while (before climbing again). When a track joins from the right, carry straight on. Continue up the well-trodden path passing a track on the left. At the intersection go right and continue uphill. At the junction with the memorial stone, turn right and, a few minutes later, follow the sign right, uphill. Then, near the barrier, go left uphill. After another steep section, reach a 'peak' with a piles of stones. Descend, ignoring a narrow path on the left (it goes to **Les Trois Fayards**, an important place of Camisard history). At a clearing enjoy some more views and continue along the ridge towards the next peak, **Signal du Bougès** (1421m). Pass an antenna and then descend with even more fine views. At the junction take the first left through the forest. When the path splits (left goes to Mijavols) keep right, signed towards 'Col du Sapet 2km'. Pass a wooden cabin/shelter and descend through forest. Go sharp left when the sign indicates and continue downhill.

You will reach a tarmac road (**Col du Sapet**, 1080m) about 1hr 30min after the junction with the memorial stone. Cross the road and continue on a dirt track. ▶ A few minutes later, when the track splits, take the left

There are number of signs with different distances here; follow the GR70 signs.

Descending to Col du Sapet with far-reaching views over the surrounding landscape

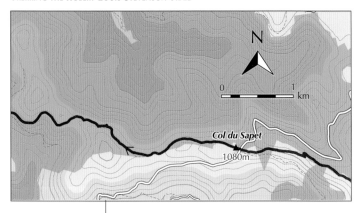

branch as the sign indicates. When it splits again, stay on the well-trodden path with fine mountain views. You will pass a track with a 'Forêt Domaniale de Ramponenche' sign, but carry straight on.

The pine tree-lined track follows the contour of the mountainside and you can see the silhouette of Mont Lozère in the distance on the right. At a junction, ignoring the track on the left, follow the sign straight on. ◄ Then, at a major junction, carry straight on downhill through thick forest. Pass a small shelter and shortly after a reservoir (**Réservoir de la Chaumette**) and a few minutes later you'll walk past a track on the left. Take a sharp right-hand turn at a junction (the GR68 goes to the left) and descend. Shortly after you pass a track on the left and continue straight on. Pine-covered mountains dominate the views as you follow the track lined with chestnut trees. At the junction go left at the 'Florac 7km' sign, and pass a stone building near the track.

Cross a stream over some rocks and soon you can admire a rocky ravine on the right. Carry straight on past a track on the right and then pass a house. Ignore a path on the left and stay on the well-trodden track. Turn left at the junction and follow the narrow tarmac road between the houses of **Bédouès** (about 2hr 30min after joining the forest track at Col du Sapet). Follow the GR70 signs

Chestnut trees grow by the track here.

through the old centre of the village, before joining rue du Couderc, which takes you to the **D998**.

Turn left onto the D998, then take the first turning right, downhill, on chemin de la Baume. Cross a bridge, and then go left, pass some houses and the tarmac road becomes gravel. The sound of rushing water coming from the River Tarn in the valley accompanies you on this section. About 20–30min after the bridge, you will come to a tarmac road. Carry straight on downhill ignoring any joining roads and tracks. At the junction turn left and cross a bridge. There is a **campsite** after the bridge. At the roundabout go left and walk along the **N106** (there is a path by the road) to **Florac**. Cross the bridge over the **River Tarnon** and follow the road to the tourist information office.

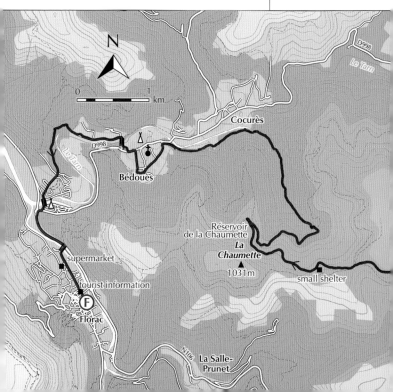

The town of **Florac**, with its medieval streets, is well visited by tourists as it makes a good base for exploring the Cévennes National Park and the nearby Gorges du Tarn.

There are a few accommodation options to choose from in Florac.

Les Tables de la Fontaine (*chambres d'hôtes*, restaurant), 31 rue du Thérond, **www.tables-de-la-fontaine.com**, tel +33 (0)4 66 65 21 73

Carline-Presbytère (*gîte d'étape*), 18 rue du Pêcher, **www.gite-florac.fr**, tel +33 (0)4 66 45 24 54

STEVENSON AND MODESTINE

After spending the night beneath chestnut trees near Le Pont-de-Montvert, Stevenson was up bright and early. He hadn't enjoyed his night under the stars as much as he had the previous night, but he had definitely started to enjoy the trek and was much taken by the beauty of his surroundings.

The route he followed on this section was different from the route followed by hikers today. Stevenson's route took him mainly alongside the River Tarn. He met and talked to some people on the way and stopped for breakfast in La Verede. He then continued to Florac where he spent the night. The locals took interest in his journey and they suggested routes for him for the following day.

Florac to Cassagnas

Start	Florac
Finish	Cassagnas
Distance	18.5km
Total ascent	645m
Total descent	485m
Time	4hr–4hr 30min
Refreshments	Supermarket, bakeries, cafés and restaurants in Florac; small snack bar near the N106 (near St-Julien-d'Arpaon); bar at the *gîte*/campsite at the end of the stage. The old railway station operates as a *gîte*, offering a meal in the evening and breakfast; you can also order packed lunch for the following day. There are no other facilities before St-Germain-de-Calberte (end of Stage 10), so get all necessary supplies in Florac

As it is a shorter and less demanding day than the previous stage, you might want to explore Florac in the morning before you set off. Leaving Florac, you walk between chestnut trees and then follow a track by the Mimente river. On a warm day you can cool your tired feet in the river near the *gîte* at Cassagnas.

From the tourist office, walk along avenue Jean Monestier to the big roundabout at the southern edge of **Florac**. At the roundabout carry straight on towards St-Jean-du-Gard, as the GR70 sign indicates. There is a towering rocky mountain above the town on the right, and the River Tarnon is down below on your left. Follow the road (**D907**) for about 10min and cross the stone bridge (**Pont de Barre**) to the left. Look out for the GR70 signs as the GR43 (also marked with red and white stripes) continues straight on. After the bridge, turn left uphill. Soon you will descend through forest and, a few minutes later, emerge onto a narrow tarmac road and turn right. There are some views of the Mimente river on your left.

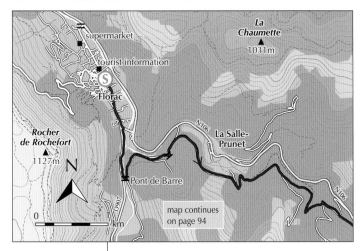

map continues
on page 94

*The narrow path
descending towards
St-Julien-d'Arpaon*

At the tarmac road junction, go left and cross the **bridge**. The towering rocky peak above Florac is on your left now. At the next intersection, turn right uphill and pass some houses. Leaving the houses behind, the road goes through forest. Ignore a road joining from the left

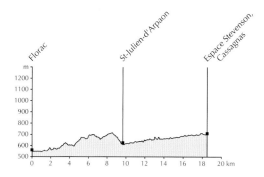

and carry straight on. Soon you can enjoy views across the valley of the hillside dotted with buildings. At the next junction, go right, uphill, and a few minutes later leave the tarmac road on a narrow path to the left and head downhill. ▶ A path joins from the left, keep right slightly uphill, and you might hear trickling water from the ravine. Pass a retaining wall on the right. Descend and soon you will cross the streambed on rocks, ignoring the path on the left and, further on, another path on the left. Emerge onto a tarmac road and head left, downhill. There are more views towards the valley as you descend on the tarmac road between chestnut trees. Pass a fountain/trough and leave the tarmac road to the right on a forest path. Cross a streambed. When the path splits, go sharp left downhill.

The forest floor is scattered with some moss-covered rocks.

Pass an old stone building in the forest. At a clearing, views open up across the valley (and then you descend through forest again). When you come to a tarmac road, cross over and continue downhill on the other side. About 2hr 15min after leaving Florac emerge onto the **N106** and turn right. Take care as you follow this busy road for a few minutes. Leave the N106 to the left on the **D20**, crossing a stone bridge. Turn right after the bridge, and walk past a warehouse, a fountain, a war memorial, the old

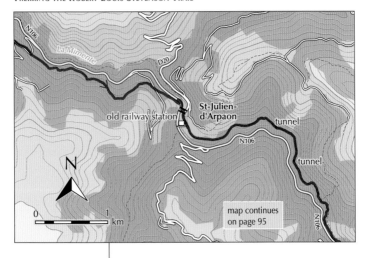

This is a flat and easy section.

railway station and, shortly after, a snack bar. Go through a gate and ignore the track on your left. Follow the old railway line with a towering mountain on your left and a dramatic gorge down below on the right. ◀ You walk through **two short tunnels** (you won't need a torch) and there are some great views. You will arrive on a tarmac road (D106) by a house about 30–40min after joining the old railway line. Cross the road and continue along its other side, then follow the old railway line through forest with a gorge on the right. Go through another **tunnel**. Emerge onto a tarmac road, turn right, pass a house and soon you will arrive at **Espace Stevenson**.

> **Cassagnas** is situated about 1.5km from the gite/ campsite at Espace Stevenson (Ancienne Gare de Cassagnas).

Espace Stevenson (*chambres d'hôtes, gîte d'étape,* camping, restaurant), Ancienne Gare (old train station), **www.relais-stevenson.fr**, annabel.larvol@gmail.com, contact@relais-stevenson.fr, tel +33 (0)4 66 45 20 34

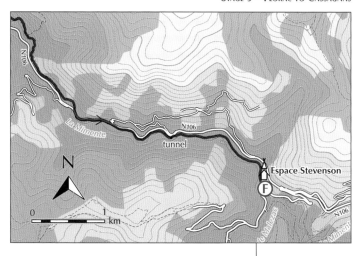

STEVENSON AND MODESTINE

The tired pair left Florac late in the afternoon and camped in the valley. The night was mild and Robert Louis Stevenson, who appeared to be enjoying his journey, spent more and more time admiring the landscape. He left his camp early and walked to Cassagnas, describing it as a remote hamlet. He happily observed that Catholics and Protestants seemed to live in peace together in the area. Stevenson made it all the way to St-Germain-de-Calberte.

The trail follows the Mimente river

STAGE 10
Cassagnas to St-Germain-de-Calberte

Start	Cassagnas
Finish	St-Germain-de-Calberte
Distance	16km
Total ascent	480m
Total descent	660m
Time	4hr
Refreshments	None along the way. There is a small shop, café, restaurant and drinking water in St-Germain-de-Calberte

This is another short section, with some fine views along the way. From the old Gare de Cassagnas ascend on forest tracks and about halfway you will reach a viewpoint (with some great views), before you start to descend through forest to St-Germain-de-Calberte. It is a pleasant, leisurely section, but some hikers prefer to walk from Florac to St-Germain-de-Calberte making it into a long and demanding day.

From the old Gare de Cassagnas (**Espace Stevenson**) follow the tarmac road, cross the bridge and continue with the stream on your left. Pass a building and leave the tarmac road to the left towards Réservoir de Boubeaux. Cross a bridge and follow the forest track slightly uphill. Ignore a track going downhill on the left, carry straight on uphill. Ignore two tracks on the left in quick succession. There are some good views framed by trees as you follow the snaking forest track on the mountainside.

Ignore a track on the right and soon you will notice the deep ravine on your right. Ascend along the forest track and, when a track joins from the left, continue straight on uphill. When you come to a junction, take the middle track downhill. At the next intersection turn left downhill as indicated on the GR70 sign (the GR70 and the GR68 share this section). You will pass the ruins of an old drystone wall in the forest. Soon you will pass

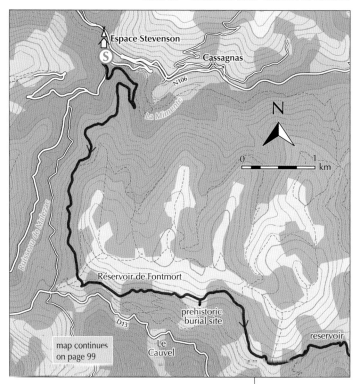

a trough and the small **Réservoir de Fontmort**. Ignore the path towards Le Cauvel on the right, and stay on the well-trodden forest track. Soon you can enjoy some magnificent mountain views on the gentle uphill section. Ignore an overgrown track and, a few minutes later, another forest track going downhill on the right; carry straight on both times. About 1hr 45min after leaving Gare de Cassagnas you will come to a viewpoint with more great mountain vistas. ▶

When the forest track splits, go right slightly downhill, as the GR70 and the GR67a signs indicate (the GR7 and GR67 go left). Enjoy the gentle descent with great views

There is prehistoric burial site about 50m off the path to the right.

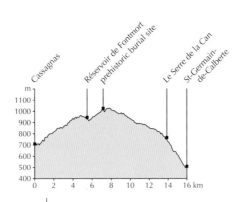

There are more chestnut trees here.

Walkers take in the views near the prehistoric burial site

as the forest track swings on the mountainside. Ignore a track joining from the right and carry straight on. When a path joins from the right, continue straight on once again, as the red and white sign indicates. ◄ Descend through the forest, past a small stone shelter at a junction, and then take the middle path downhill towards **Le Serre de la Can**. At a junction take the right branch and join a wide track and continue straight on downhill. Some views open up on the left as the track swings on the

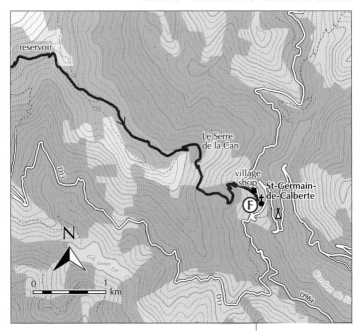

mountainside. At the junction with a **reservoir**, go sharp left and, about 100m later, leave this track to the right and head downhill. When the path splits by a fenced area, carry straight on and at the end of the fenced area continue straight on downhill.

Descend on the rocky path with views of tree-covered mountains. At a junction go left downhill. Ignoring a track on the left, carry straight on. Zigzag downhill and, arriving at a forest track, go right. Continue downhill with views of the mountainside dotted with houses. Pass a *gîte* and arrive at a minor tarmac road, keep right and follow the road to the centre of **St-Germain-de-Calberte**.

Au Figuier des Cévennes (*gîte d'étape*, restaurant), **www.gite-etape-cevennes.fr**, resa@aufiguierdesce-vennes.com, tel +33 (0)6 66 36 53 29

Prehistoric burial site and its standing stone with the mountains of the Cévennes in the background

La Lune Rousse (*gîte d'étape*, *table d'hôtes*), **www.lalunerousse-cevennes.fr**, lalunerousse.cevennes@yahoo.fr, tel +33 (0)6 83 77 16 45

Alternative accommodation in the valley, about 3km from the village centre, is available at La Ferme de Lancizolle, **www.causses-cevennes.com/ferme-lanci-zolle**, lafermedelancizolle@gmail.com, tel +33 (0)4 66 45 92 82. In high season (between mid July and mid August) they might only take bookings for a minimum of two nights.

STEVENSON AND MODESTINE

Stevenson dined in Cassagnas and then, as he continued his walk, he met a very old shepherd who mistook him for a pedlar. The shepherd directed him towards St-Germain-de-Calberte. He then walked alone without seeing anyone else all afternoon. Stevenson and Modestine reached St-Germain-de-Calberte in darkness and he spent the night in the village inn.

STAGE 11
St-Germain-de-Calberte to St-Jean-du-Gard

Start	St-Germain-de-Calberte
Finish	St-Jean-du-Gard
Distance	23km
Total ascent	745m
Total descent	1055m
Time	6hr
Refreshments	Small shop, café and restaurant in St-Germain-de-Calberte; café, restaurant and shop in St-Étienne-Vallée-Française mid-stage; cafés, restaurants, shops and bakeries in St-Jean-du-Gard

Robert Louis Stevenson finished his journey in St-Jean-du-Gard, so this is the last day you will be following in his footsteps. You might feel a bit sad to be nearing the end of the trail but there are some excellent views to brighten up your day. From St-Germain-de-Calberte you follow forest tracks among chestnut trees and then, from St-Étienne-Vallée-Française, you climb with excellent views before descending to St-Jean-du-Gard.

Follow the red and white signs through and out of the village and then turn right off the main road near the **recycling area** onto a narrow tarmac road. Ignore two tracks on the right as you ascend through forest. Leave this narrow tarmac road on a bend and follow the sign straight on. Soon pass a house and follow the stony forest track. ▶ About 10min after passing the recycling area, you will come to the **D13**; cross over and continue downhill. There are some fine views on the left and you can see St-Germain-de-Calberte's houses clinging to the hillside.

Pass some gardens and houses and, at a junction, continue straight on downhill. Ignore any joining dirt tracks and paths from either side, and take in the views. ▶ The track follows the contour of the forested

Chestnut trees populate the hillside here.

On the right, a fallen tree with curved tendrils looks like a modern artwork.

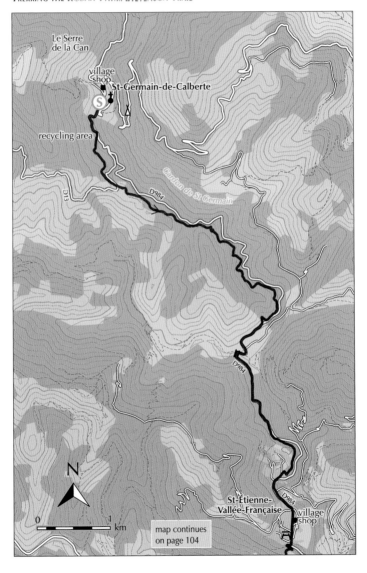

Le Serre
de la Can

village
shop

St-Germain-de-Calberte

S

recycling area

D13

Garden de St Germain

D984

D984

N

0   1
|_____| km

St-Étienne-
Vallée-Française

village
shop

map continues
on page 104

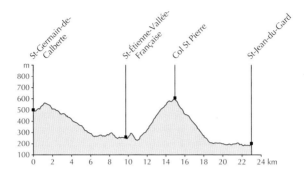

mountainside. Ignoring a track on the left, continue on the well-trodden path and enjoy more views at the clearing. At a junction, take the left branch and descend on the stony path. Ignore a dirt track on the right and then, immediately after, another one on the left, and carry straight on downhill. A valley comes into view with mountains in the background.

About 1hr 20min after leaving St-Germain-de-Calberte you will arrive at the main road (**D984**). Go right, cross the bridge and continue on the D984. There are gîtes (Les Mus Stevenson and La Ferme de Patience) along the road. Turn right off the road onto a stony path that leads uphill, as the red and white sign indicates. Pass some buildings and continue on the mountainside. The track becomes a tarmac road by a house and, a few minutes later rejoins the D984. Turn right into **St-Étienne-Vallée-Française** about 2hr 10min after leaving St-Germain-de-Calberte. ▶

Follow the road through the village and pass a picnic area near the Mairie (town hall) and tourist office. Just after the village, turn right off the D984 onto a narrow road (as the red and white sign indicates). Ignore a track on the right, continue uphill and the tarmac road soon becomes a forest track by a house. As you descend

In St-Étienne-Vallée-Française you'll find a gîte, café, restaurant, drinking water and two small shops.

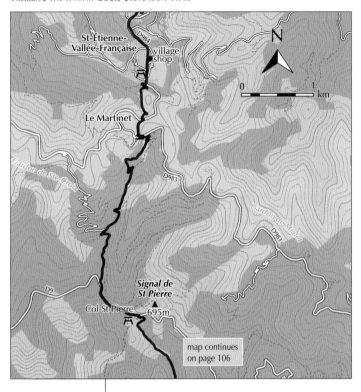

map continues
on page 106

Notice some labelled
plants by the path.

you can enjoy some views towards the mountains and
the valley with a bridge. When you arrive at a road junction, and keep right along the **D983**. Cross the bridge
over the **Gardon de Ste Croix** river (near Le Martinet restaurant). After the bridge, turn right off the D983 onto a
stony uphill path. At a junction go right uphill with more
views of the valley and the river. ◄ Ignore a path joining
from the left and stay on the well-trodden path. There are
great views of the mountains and exposed rocks dominating the scenery on the left. Pass an old retaining wall as
you ascend through forest. Emerge onto a forest track and
bear right; about 100m later pass a track on the right.

When the path splits, keep left slightly uphill with some views of the mountains and a valley. Ignoring a track on the right, turn sharp left uphill on the well-trodden path. Also pass another track on the right and continue straight on. The trail then levels out for a while before heading uphill again. When the track splits, take the right-hand branch uphill and enjoy the views of the mountains. About 1hr after crossing the Gardon de Ste Croix river, you emerge onto the **D9** and go left. There is a picnic site by the road (**Col St Pierre**).

Look out for the GR70 signs and turn right off the D9 onto a narrow path, where the guardrail starts after the picnic site. It is a steep descent on a rocky path. Zigzag downhill and soon you will be descending through forest. Turn left downhill by some buildings and continue on the stony path, with views of the mountains. The dirt track becomes a tarmac road as you curve downhill. At a small junction (**Rancassette**), carry straight on, as the 'St-Jean-du-Gard 5km' sign indicates. Ignoring a dirt track on your left, continue downhill. Turn left when you get to the **D907**. Leave this road on a path to the right leading down to the river with a bridge. Continue parallel to the

Rocky path above the Gardon de Ste Croix

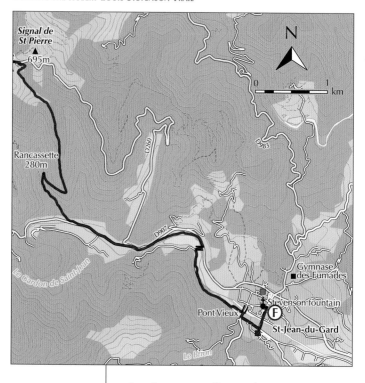

road, and soon you will rejoin the D907. Shortly after turn right off the tarmac road again, as indicated on the sign, and walk along the river. Turn right, cross the bridge, bear left after the bridge (there is *gîte* on the right) and walk past some gardens and buildings. Walk through forest by the river until you reach a tarmac road by buildings. Head towards the bridge. Go under the bridge (**Pont Vieux**) and turn right then left at a junction towards the 'Centre Ville'. Follow that road to the train station, then turn left and cross the bridge. There are restaurants, bars, cafés, a post office, tourist office and shops in **St-Jean-du-Gard**. Look out for the fountain on the left commemorating Stevenson's journey. ◀

Further down the road, there is also a plaque in a park near the post office building.

In the 19th century, the silk industry played an important role in the economy of **St-Jean-du-Gard**. Today, however, the main income is from tourism. The heritage railway attracts thousands of tourists every year.

Auberge du Peras (hotel and restaurant), route de Nîmes, **www.aubergeduperas.com**, aubergeduperas@free.fr, tel +33 (0)4 66 85 35 94

Hôtel Les Bellugues, 13 rue Pelet de la Lozère, **www.hotel-bellugues.com**, contactbellugues@orange.fr, tel +33 (0)4 66 85 15 33

Fountain in St-Jean-du-Gard commemorating Stevenson's journey

STEVENSON AND MODESTINE

Stevenson liked the quiet St-Germain-de-Calberte, and he took his time in the morning. He had coffee and then had lunch with some local Catholics, so it was afternoon by the time he left the village. He walked through St-Étienne-Vallée-Française (just as hikers do today) and climbed Col St Pierre. He wanted to enjoy some views before nightfall; however, the exhausted Modestine and Stevenson only reached St-Jean-du-Gard late in the evening, well after dark.

STAGE 12
St-Jean-du-Gard to Alès

Start	St-Jean-du-Gard
Finish	Alès
Distance	25.5km
Total ascent	950m
Total descent	1010m
Time	7hr 30min–8hr
Refreshments	Cafés, restaurants, shops and bakeries in St-Jean-du-Gard and in Alès, but none along the way

Robert Louis Stevenson took a coach from St-Jean-du-Gard to Alès and, while some walkers do the same, many choose to walk this last – sometimes difficult but very scenic – section. The trail has recently been altered between Mialet and Alès and is now a signposted section, so you can follow GR70 signs all the way to Alès.

Walk along place de la Révolution with the Mairie (town hall) on your right. At the end of the street at the big junction (with the bus station on your left) carry straight on towards Mialet. There is a GR61 sign as well as the GR70 sign. Turn right uphill towards the **Gymnase des Fumades**, and soon you will pass a *gîte*. Continue uphill, ignoring any side roads (towards the houses). At the signposted junction (Chemin de Luc, alt 266m), turn left towards Mialet as the GR61 and the GR70 signs indicate. Curve uphill on the narrow, signposted road, ignoring a dirt track on the left. Soon you have some mountain views. At the junction, go right as the red and white sign indicates and follow the GR61 and GR70 signs through pine forest. Ignoring a track on the left, continue right as the GR sign indicates. Pass a house then, at **La Borie** junction, take the right branch (GR61) towards Montezorgues and then turn left off the tarmac road onto a stony path on the forested mountainside. You can enjoy some fine

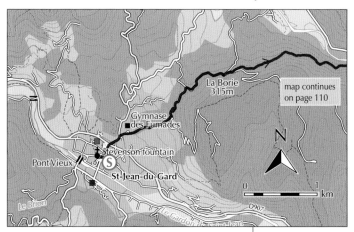

map continues on page 110

views framed by trees. As you descend through forest, you will get a glimpse of the **Gardon de Mialet** river down in the valley and there is a towering rock on the right. The path becomes a tarmac road by a house/*gîte*; follow it downhill between houses and cross the bridge (**Pont des Camisards**) about 1hr 30min after leaving St-Jean-du-Gard.

Emerge onto the **D50** and go right to **Mialet**. Turn left onto the first street (rue des Oliviers) just before you get

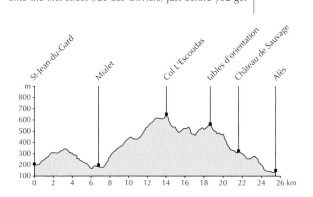

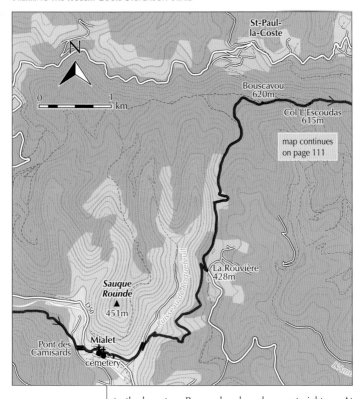

Tree-covered mountains dominate the views as you climb the mountainside.

to the bus stop. Pass a church and carry straight on. At the junction (Le Temple, alt 189m) carry straight on and pass another church. At rue Jacques Bernard (alt 180m), go left on a narrow road towards L'Escoudas (a GR70 sign marks this). Follow the stony, grassy path, past the **cemetery**, then cross a tarmac road and continue straight on a narrow path between drystone walls. Ignore a path on the left, and carry straight on, parallel to the road. Emerge onto the tarmac road and turn left (there is a GR70 sign), following the road past some houses. About 150m later cross the stone bridge on the right and continue uphill on a stony path. ◄

Ignore an overgrown path on the left and continue uphill. Arrive at a forest track junction (**La Rouvière** 428m) and take a sharp left towards L'Escoudas, indicated on the GR70 sign. Follow the stony track uphill, passing an overgrown track on the left, another small path on the

Gardon de Mialet river

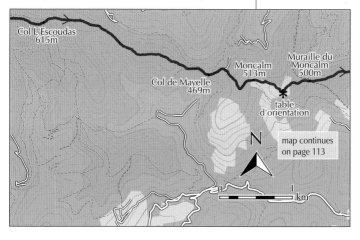

map continues on page 113

left and a track on the right. At a junction (**Bouscavou**) keep right towards Moncalm, as the GR70 sign indicates.

At L'Escoudas, turn left off the dirt track onto a path, as the red and white 'GR70 Moncalm 4.1km' sign indicates. Continue on the narrow path uphill and then soon descend with some great mountain views. When you arrive at a dirt track (**Col de L'Escoudas**, 615m), cross over and head downhill, as indicated on the red and white sign. As you descend you can spot St-Paul-la-Coste's houses in the valley. Ignore the faint paths on either side of the track as you follow the ridge. Shortly after descend on a narrow forest path and, when it splits, go left. A few minutes later when its splits again, turn left once more. Ignore a path on the right, and follow the sign to the left. Great views open up towards the mountains and the valley.

When you get to a forest path, turn left and, at a dirt track junction (**Col de Mayelle**, 469m), take the second path from the right towards the **table d'orientation**, as the red and white and red and yellow signs indicate. The path soon becomes a surfaced road. Carry straight on when the dirt track bends and head uphill with some great views. Ignore a track on the left and, passing a house, follow the signs through the forest. At a junction (**Moncalm**, alt 513m) take the second trail from the left towards 'Notre Dame de Rochebelle GR70'. Climb onto rocks to enjoy some more great views. Then walk along the ridge and take in the views from the three viewpoints. ◄ From one of the viewpoints you can see your destination: Alès. Descend steeply between trees and look out for the red and white signs as there is a network of paths here. At a junction (**Muraille du Moncalm**, alt 500m) go right, as the red and white signs indicate, and descend through forest. After a steep downhill section, you will arrive at a dirt track (**Valmalette**, alt 345m) and bear left. Carry straight on at the **Château de Sauvage** junction (but first see the ruins of the château on the right.)

When the track splits, turn right downhill. At Sous Château de Sauvage junction (alt 307m) carry straight on and, a few metres later, at the iron cross **Croix de**

On a clear day if you look back, you can still make out the silhouette of Mont Lozère; this is your chance to take a last glimpse of the mountains you have traversed over the past few days.

The hidden ruins of Château de Sauvage

Sauvage, turn right off the dirt track and follow the narrow path through forest. ▶ At the **Trépeloup** junction go left as the GR sign indicates. Follow the forest track and ignore the unmarked path. At a clearing, keep right and at a junction (Terre Rouge) go right and descend with

Stay on the path here as the ground is dotted with huge cracks and deep holes!

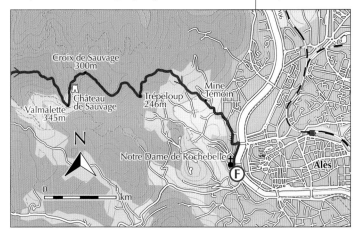

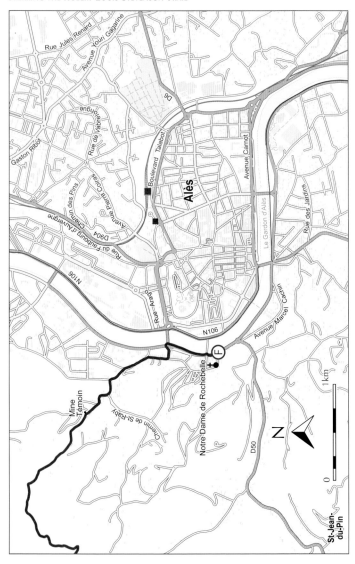

Rue Jules Renard
Avenue Youri Gagarine
D6
Rue de l'abreuvoir
Gaston Ribot
Avenue Pierre Curie Colorès
Chemin des Pins
Rue du Faubourg d'Auvergne
D904
N106
Boulevard Talabot
Alès
Avenue Carnot
Le Gardon d'Alès
Rue des Jardins
Rue Aragon
N106
Avenue Marcel Cachin
Mine Témoin
Chemin de St-Raby
Notre Dame de Rochebelle
F
D50
St-Jean-du-Pin
N
1 km
0

views towards Alès. Walk alongside a retaining wall, ignoring a path on the right. Cross a tarmac road and continue to follow the path. Pass the old mine museum (**Mine Témoin**) and carry on downhill. When you arrive at a tarmac road (Cité Ste Marie, 168m) by houses, continue right downhill on the tarmac road. At a junction keep left (you can still spot some GR signs here) and you will arrive at a T-junction; turn right towards **Alès** Centre Ville. Follow this road ignoring any joining streets and go left on rue du Capitaine Albert. At the roundabout keep right and continue with the **Gardon d'Alès** river on your left. Follow the last few GR70 signs to **Notre Dame de Rochebelle** church, where the Robert Louis Stevenson Trail ends.

Hôtel Durand, 3 boulevard Anatole France, **www.hotel-durand-ales.com**, ales.hotel.durand@gmail.com, tel +33 (0)4 66 86 28 94

ALÈS

You can explore the small town of Alès in an afternoon. The Roman Catholic Cathedral, dedicated to St John the Baptist, was built in the 17th century after Alès – once the centre of the Huguenots – was taken by Louis XIII. There is also a 17th-century fort that served as a prison for Protestants.

The area was an important coal-mining centre in the 19th century but mining gradually declined in the 1960s and ceased in 1985.

There are plenty of cafés and restaurants in Alès where you can treat yourself at the end of the trek.

To reach the train station from Notre Dame de Rochebelle church, retrace your steps to the bridge. Cross the bridge and turn left, and at the next roundabout turn right onto Quai Boissier de Sauvages (road). At the next roundabout continue on Boulevard Louis Blanc. At the next roundabout turn left onto Avenue Général de Gaulle. Follow this road for about 500 metres to the station.

APPENDIX A
Useful contacts and information

Many sites have an English version. For French-only sites, your browser may offer a translation if you are not a French speaker.

If phoning a French number from overseas, you will need to include the international dialling code 00 33 and omit the first zero of the number. So for French number 01 23 45 67 89 you would dial 00 33 1 23 45 67 89.

Useful websites

GR70
GR70 Robert Louis Stevenson Trail
www.gr70-stevenson.com/en/trail.htm

Le Chemin de Robert Louis Stevenson (French site)
www.chemin-stevenson.org

Robert Louis Stevenson
www.robert-louis-stevenson.org

Tourist information
Causses Cévennes
www.causses-cevennes.com

Cévennes National Park
www.cevennes-parcnational.fr

Cévennes Tourism
www.cevennes-tourisme.fr

FFRandonnée (French hiking association)
www.ffrandonnee.fr

Gard Tourism
www.gardtourism.com

Lozère Tourism
www.en.lozere-tourisme.com

Transport

Air
British Airways (from London to Lyon)
www.britishairways.com

Easyjet (from London to Lyon)
www.easyjet.com

Ryanair (from London to Nîmes)
www.ryanair.com

Rhône Express (Lyon airport tramlink)
www.rhonexpress.fr/en

Bus and train
La Région (regional buses)
www.laregion.fr

SNCF (trains)
ww.sncf.com/en

Trainline (trains and buses in the UK and Europe)
www.thetrainline.com

Accommodation
www.airbnb.co.uk

www.booking.com

www.gites-refuges.com

www.hotelscombined.com

www.travelsupermarket.com

Donkey hire
www.aneazimut.com

www.artsetnature.fr

www.rando-ane.fr

www.lemasdesanes.com

Luggage transfer
www.stevenson-transport.fr

www.transbagages.com

Tourist offices
Alès
Place de l'Hôtel de Ville
tel +33 (0)4 66 52 32 15

Florac
33 avenue Jean Monestier
tel +33 (0)4 66 45 01 14

La Bastide-Puylaurent
Place de L'Église
tel +33 (0)4 66 46 12 83

Langogne
15 boulevard des Capucins
tel +33 (0)4 66 69 01 38

Le Monastier-sur-Gazeille
Place du Vallat
tel +33 (0)4 71 08 37 76

Le Pont-de-Montvert
Le Quai
tel +33 (0)4 66 45 81 94

Le Puy-en-Velay
2 place du Clauzel
tel +33 (0)4 71 09 38 41

Pradelles
Place de la Halle
tel +33 (0)4 71 00 82 65

St-Jean-du-Gard
5 rue de l'industrie, Maison Rouge
tel +33 (0)4 66 85 32 11

APPENDIX B
Accommodation

Le Monastier-sur-Gazeille
File dans ta chambre (*gîte d'étape*)
25 rue St-Pierre
filedanschambre@outlook.fr
tel +33 (0)6 74 59 22 72
www.filedanstachambre.monsite-orange.fr

Auberge les Acacias
1 rond-point des Acacias
aubergelesacacias@orange.fr
tel +33 (0)4 71 08 38 11
www.aubergelesacacias.fr

Le Bouchet-St-Nicolas
L'Arrestadou (*chambres d'hôtes, gîte d'étape, table d'hôtes*)
Route de Cayres
tel +33 (0)4 71 57 35 34
www.larrestadou.fr

La Retirade (*gîte d'étape, table d'hôtes*)
Place de l'Église
contact@gitelaretirade.com
tel +33 (0)6 29 42 61 50
www.gitelaretirade.com

Langogne
Hôtel du Languedoc
6 avenue du Maréchal Joffre
hoteldulanguedoc.langogne@gmail.com
tel +33 (0)4 66 46 31 08
www.hoteldulanguedoc-langogne.com

Modest'inn (*chambres d'hôtes, table d'hôtes*)
2 rue de la Honde
modestinn.48@gmail.com
tel +33 (0)4 66 46 48 33
www.modestinn-chambres-dhotes.fr

Cheylard-l'Évêque
Le Refuge du Moure (*chambres d'hôtes, gîte d'étape, table d'hôtes*)
info@lozere-gite.com
tel +33 (0)4 66 69 03 21
www.lozere-gite.com

Hôtel de France
Chaudeyrac
info@hoteldefrance-lozere.com
tel +33 (0)4 66 47 91 00
www.hoteldefrance-lozere.com

La Bastide-Puylaurent
Hôtel La Grand Halt
Rue des Tilleuls
tel +33 (0)4 66 46 00 35
www.hotel-lagrandhalte.fr

Hôtel Les Genêts
Rue des Tilleuls
hotelgenets@hotmail.fr
tel +33 (0)4 66 46 00 13

Le Bleymard
La Remise (*hotel*)
contact@hotel-laremise.com
tel +33 (0)4 66 48 65 80
www.hotel-laremise.com

La Combette (*chambres d'hôtes, table d'hôtes*)
lacombette@hotmail.fr
tel +33 (0)6 86 34 01 86
www.lacombette.com

Le Pont-de-Montvert
Gîtes du Chastel
Quartier de la Moline
gitesduchastel@cevennes-gites.com

tel +33 (0)6 80 21 14 10
www.cevennes-gites.com

Auberges des Cévennes
lescevennes@orange.fr
tel +33 (0)4 66 45 80 01
www.auberge-des-cevennes.com

Florac
Les Tables de la Fontaine (*chambres d'hôtes*, restaurant)
31 rue du Thérond
tel +33 (0)4 66 65 21 73
www.tables-de-la-fontaine.com

Carline-Presbytère (*gîte d'étape*)
18 rue du Pêcher
tel +33 (0)4 66 45 24 54
www.gite-florac.fr

Cassagnas
Espace Stevenson (*chambres d'hôtes, gîte d'étape*, camping, restaurant)
Ancienne Gare (old train station)
annabel.larvol@gmail.comcontact@relais-stevenson.fr
tel +33 (0)4 66 45 20 34
www.relais-stevenson.fr

St-Germain-de-Calberte
Au Figuier des Cévennes (*gîte d'étape*, restaurant)
resa@aufiguierdescevennes.com
tel +33 (0)6 66 36 53 29
www.gite-etape-cevennes.fr

La Lune Rousse (*gîte d'étape, table d'hôtes*)
lalunerousse.cevennes@yahoo.fr
tel +33 (0)6 83 77 16 45
www.lalunerousse-cevennes.fr

La Ferme de Lancizolle (minimum of two nights in high season)
About 3km from the village centre
lafermedelancizolle@gmail.com
tel +33 (0)4 66 45 92 82
www.causses-cevennes.com/ferme-lancizolle

St-Jean-du-Gard
Auberge du Peras (hotel and restaurant)
Route de Nîmes
aubergeduperas@free.fr
tel +33 (0)4 66 85 35 94
www.aubergeduperas.com

Hôtel Les Bellugues
13 rue Pelet de la Lozère
contactbellugues@orange.fr
tel +33 (0)4 66 85 15 33
www.hotel-bellugues.com

Alès
Hôtel Durand
3 boulevard Anatole France
ales.hotel.durand@gmail.com
tel +33 (0)4 66 86 28 94
www.hotel-durand-ales.com

APPENDIX C
Campsites

Le Puy-en-Velay
Camping de Bouthezard
Chemin de Bouthezard
Le Puy-en-Velay
tel +33 (0)4 71 09 55 09
www.aquadis-loisirs.com/en/
camping-bouthezard

Camping de Coubon
Route de Souchiol
Coubon
tel +33 (0)6 80 96 89 00

Le Monastier-sur-Gazeille
Gîte et Camping l'Estela
Route du moulin de Savin
Le Monastier-sur-Gazeille
tel +33 (0)4 71 03 82 24
www.campingestela.fr

Goudet
Camping au Bord de l'Eau
Le Chambon
Goudet
tel +33 (0)4 71 57 16 82
www.campingauborddeleau.com

Le Bouchet-St-Nicolas
Municipal camping
Route du Stade
Le Bouchet-St-Nicolas
tel +33 (0)4 71 57 32 22

Pradelles
Le Rocher de Grelet
Avenue de Langogne
Pradelles
tel +33 (0)4 71 00 03 72

Langogne
Camping La Cigale de l'Allier
9 Route de St-Alban en Montagne
Langogne
tel +33 (0)6 80 15 96 32
www.lacigaledelallier.fr

Fouzilhac
La Halte de Fouzilhac
Fouzilhac
tel +33 (0)4 66 69 22 62
www.haltedefouzilhac.fr

La Bastide-Puylaurent
Camping de l'Allier
Route de Mende
La Bastide-Puylaurent
tel +33 (0)4 66 46 04 06
www.camping-de-lallier.fr

Le Bleymard
Camping Municipal la Gazelle
Route de Villefort
Le Bleymard
tel +33 (0)4 66 48 60 48

Finiels
Camping la Barette
Finiels
tel +33 (0)4 66 45 82 16
lucile.camping@gmail.com

Le Pont-de-Montvert
Camping Municipal
Le Pont-de-Montvert
tel +33 (0)4 66 45 82 88
www.campingmunicipal-
pontdemontvert.fr

Bédouès
Camping Chon du Tarn
Bédouès
tel +33 (0)4 66 45 09 14
www.camping-chondutarn.com

Florac
Camping du Pont Neuf
N106, Le Pont Neuf
Florac
tel +33 (0)4 66 32 42 55
www.campingdupontneuf.com

Flower Camping Le Pont du Tarn
D998
Florac
tel +33 (0)4 66 45 18 26
www.camping-florac.com

Camping Le Val des Cévennes
5 route de Mende
Florac
tel +33 (0)4 66 31 34 20
www.levaldescevennes.com

Cassagnas
Espace Stevenson (hotel, *gîte*, camping)
Ancienne Gare
Cassagnas
tel +33 (0)4 66 45 20 34
www.relais-stevenson.fr

St-Germain-de-Calberte
Camping Le Garde
Le Garde
St-Germain-de-Calberte
tel +33 (0)6 66 36 53 29
www.cevennes-voyages.com

St-Étienne-Vallée-Française
Le Martinet Camping and Gîte
La Farre
St-Étienne-Vallée-Française
tel +33 (0)4 66 45 74 88
www.village-vacances-cevennes.com

St-Jean-du-Gard
Camping Le Petit Baigneur
Les Deux Chemins
St-Jean-du-Gard
tel +33 (0)6 87 69 01 63
www.camping-le-petit-baigneur.fr

Camping Mas de la Cam
Route de St André de Valborgne
St-Jean-du-Gard
tel +33 (0)4 66 85 12 02
www.camping-cevennes.info

Mialet
Camping Les Plans
Les Plans (D50)
Mialet
tel +33 (0)4 66 85 02 46
www.camping-les-plans.fr

Alès
Camping La Croix Clémentine
1313 route de la Baume
Cendras (nr Alès)
tel +33 (0)4 66 86 52 69
www.clementine.fr

APPENDIX D
French–English glossary

French	English
Greetings	
bonjour	good morning
bonsoir	good evening
Transport	
arrêt de bus	bus stop
billet	ticket
gare	station (railway)
horaire de bus	bus timetable
Accommodation	
camping	campsite
chambre	room
chambre d'hôtes	guestroom
gîte	guest house/ dormitory
hôtel	hotel
tente	tent
Food and drink	
bon appétit	enjoy your meal
boulangerie	bakery
café	coffee
déjeuner	lunch
dîner/souper	dinner/supper
eau	water
eau potable	drinking water
fromage	cheese
pain	bread

French	English
petit déjeuner	breakfast
vin	wine
In town	
école	school
église	church
mairie	town hall
marché	market
musée	museum
office de tourisme	tourist information office
route	road
rue	street
supermarché	supermarket
On the trail	
âne	donkey
ascension	ascent
carte	map
chemin	path
col de montagne	col (mountain pass)
colline	hill
crête	ridge
élévation	elevation
fleuve	river/stream
forêt	forest
grande randonnée (GR)	long-distance trail

French	English
montagne	mountain
pic	peak
piste	track/trail
pont	bridge
privé/privée	private
randonnée	hike
randonneur/ randonneuse	hiker
refuge	shelter
rivière	river
rocher	rock

French	English
ruisseau	brook/stream
sentier	path
sommet	peak/summit
vallée	valley
Emergencies	
ambulance	ambulance
hôpital	hospital
police	police
pompiers	fire brigade
urgence	emergency

DOWNLOAD THE ROUTES
IN GPX FORMAT

GPX files for all the routes in this guide are available to download from:

www.cicerone.co.uk/918/GPX

You should be able to use these files on a GPS device or your preferred GPS app on your desktop or smartphone.

When you go to this link, you will be asked for your email address and where you purchased the guide, and have the option to subscribe to the Cicerone e-newsletter.

www.cicerone.co.uk

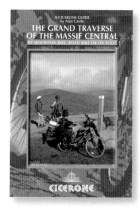
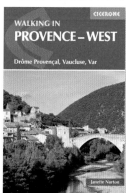
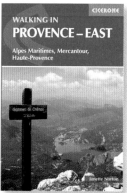

INTERNATIONAL LISTING OF CICERONE GUIDES

INTERNATIONAL CHALLENGES, COLLECTIONS AND ACTIVITIES

Canyoning in the Alps
Europe's High Points
The Via Francigena Canterbury to Rome – Part 2

AFRICA

Kilimanjaro
The High Atlas
Walking in the Drakensberg
Walks and Scrambles in the Moroccan Anti-Atlas

ALPS CROSS-BORDER ROUTES

100 Hut Walks in the Alps
Alpine Ski Mountaineering Vol 1 – Western Alps
Alpine Ski Mountaineering Vol 2 – Central and Eastern Alps
Chamonix to Zermatt
The Karnischer Hohenweg
The Tour of the Bernina
Tour of Monte Rosa
Tour of the Matterhorn
Trail Running – Chamonix and the Mont Blanc region
Trekking in the Alps
Trekking in the Silvretta and Ratikon Alps
Trekking Munich to Venice
Trekking the Tour of Mont Blanc
Walking in the Alps

PYRENEES AND FRANCE/SPAIN CROSS-BORDER ROUTES

Shorter Treks in the Pyrenees
The GR10 Trail
The GR11 Trail
The Pyrenean Haute Route
The Pyrenees
Walks and Climbs in the Pyrenees

AUSTRIA

Innsbruck Mountain Adventures
The Adlerweg
Trekking in Austria's Hohe Tauern
Trekking in the Stubai Alps
Trekking in the Zillertal Alps
Walking in Austria
Walking in the Salzkammergut: the Austrian Lake District

EASTERN EUROPE

The Danube Cycleway Vol 2
The High Tatras
The Mountains of Romania
Walking in Bulgaria's National Parks
Walking in Hungary

FRANCE, BELGIUM AND LUXEMBOURG

Chamonix Mountain Adventures
Cycle Touring in France
Cycling London to Paris
Cycling the Canal de la Garonne
Cycling the Canal du Midi
Mont Blanc Walks
Mountain Adventures in the Maurienne
Short Treks on Corsica
The GR20 Corsica
The GR5 Trail
The GR5 Trail – Benelux and Lorraine
The GR5 Trail – Vosges and Jura
The Grand Traverse of the Massif Central
The Loire Cycle Route
The Moselle Cycle Route
The River Rhone Cycle Route
The Robert Louis Stevenson Trail
The Way of St James – Le Puy to the Pyrenees
Tour of the Queyras
Trekking the Robert Louis Stevenson Trail
Vanoise Ski Touring
Via Ferratas of the French Alps
Walking in Corsica
Walking in Provence – East
Walking in Provence – West
Walking in the Ardennes
Walking in the Auvergne
Walking in the Brianconnais
Walking in the Dordogne
Walking in the Haute Savoie: North
Walking in the Haute Savoie: South

GERMANY

Hiking and Cycling in the Black Forest

The Danube Cycleway Vol 1
The Rhine Cycle Route
The Westweg
Walking in the Bavarian Alps

HIMALAYA

Annapurna
Everest: A Trekker's Guide
The Mount Kailash Trek
Trekking in Bhutan
Trekking in Ladakh
Trekking in the Himalaya

IRELAND

The Wild Atlantic Way and Western Ireland

ITALY

Italy's Sibillini National Park
Shorter Walks in the Dolomites
Ski Touring and Snowshoeing in the Dolomites
The Way of St Francis
Trekking in the Apennines
Trekking in the Dolomites
Trekking the Giants' Trail: Alta Via 1 through the Italian Pennine Alps
Via Ferratas of the Italian Dolomites Vols 1&2
Walking and Trekking in the Gran Paradiso
Walking in Abruzzo
Walking in Italy's Cinque Terre
Walking in Italy's Stelvio National Park
Walking in Sardinia
Walking in Sicily
Walking in the Dolomites
Walking in Tuscany
Walking in Umbria
Walking Lake Como and Maggiore
Walking Lake Garda and Iseo
Walking on the Amalfi Coast
Walking the Via Francigena Pilgrim Route – Part 3
Walks and Treks in the Maritime Alps

For full information on all our guides, books and eBooks, visit our website:
www.cicerone.co.uk

Explore the world with Cicerone

**walking • trekking • mountaineering • climbing • mountain biking •
cycling • via ferratas • scrambling • trail running • skills and techniques**

For over 50 years, Cicerone have built up an outstanding collection of nearly 400 guides, inspiring all sorts of amazing experiences.

www.cicerone.co.uk – where adventures begin

- Our **website** is a treasure-trove for every outdoor adventurer. You can buy books or read inspiring articles and trip reports, get technical advice, check for updates, and view videos, photographs and mapping for routes and treks.

- **Register this book** or any other Cicerone guide in your member's library on our website and you can choose to automatically access updates and GPX files for your books, if available.

- Our **fortnightly newsletters** will update you on new publications and articles and keep you informed of other news and events. You can also follow us on Facebook, Twitter and Instagram.

We hope you have enjoyed using this guidebook. If you have any comments you would like to share, please contact us using the form on our website or via email, so that we can provide the best experience for future customers.

CICERONE

Juniper House, Murley Moss Business Village, Oxenholme Road, Kendal LA9 7RL

✉ info@cicerone.co.uk   cicerone.co.uk